COMP
LAW in the
EUROPEAN
COMMUNITY

COMPETITION LAW in the EUROPEAN COMMUNITY

2nd Edition

David M Jacobs
and
Jack Stewart-Clark

KOGAN PAGE

First published in 1990
Second edition published in 1991

Kogan Page Limited
120 Pentonville Road
London N1 9JN

British Library Cataloguing in Publication Data
A CIP record for this book is available from the British Library.

ISBN 0 7494 0502 3

Typeset by J&L Composition Ltd, Filey, North Yorkshire
Printed and bound in Great Britain by Biddles Ltd,
Guildford and Kings Lynn

Contents

Foreword

Throughout its history the Commission has been dismantling barriers to trade. We are now in a phase of intense activity which will complete this process, in order to create a Single European Market after 1992.

We have paid a high price for segmenting the Community into individual domestic markets. The Cecchini Report estimated this loss at between 4.3 per cent to 6.4 per cent of Community Gross Domestic Product (GDP) or 200 billion ECU in 1988, and fragmented markets have meant chronic decline in the competitiveness of some of our firms. Protected by barriers to trade, they have lost their competitive edge and sense of enterprise. These same barriers have denied opportunities to new entrants, whose entrepreneurial skills have been smothered. The 1992 programme is designed to reverse these conditions. It will reduce the burdensome costs of administration and technical compliance, whilst liberalizing previously closed markets.

One of the most beneficial aspects of the Single European Market is the widening of choice it will provide to all consumers. The entry of new firms, the opening of markets and the easing of trade will all add to the range of goods and services available to every customer in the Community. Diversity and choice are the natural consequences of the Single European Market. It follows that firms will need to compete more strenuously. They will need to innovate, watch their costs, tend to the quality of their products and enhance the skills of their employees. Competition provides benefits to all. Diversity, choice and competition will be the dominant features of the European landscape after 1992.

This brings me to the matter of acquisitions and mergers. There is little point in the Commission's efforts to dismantle impediments to competition and trade if businesses build new ones. The 1992 programme is markedly pro-competitive but some mergers and acquisitions may be anti-competitive. In order to avoid having less choice, narrowed diversity and reduced competition, we have to be able to permit mergers that strengthen industry without damaging competition, but prevent mergers which diminish effective choice in a damaging way.

Mergers and acquisitions occur in as disparate activities as football clubs and defence electronics companies. Most mergers are between firms from the same country. Increasingly, mergers involve companies in more than one Member State or companies from Member States and non-members. The Commission's figures for 1987/88 show that there were over 320 national mergers, 146 Community mergers and 91 involving Community companies with those from other countries. Of the 383 mergers in industry that we recorded, 70 per cent involved firms whose combined turnover exceeded 1,000 million ECU. In the service sector over 40 per cent of mergers surpassed this figure. Our latest research indicates the total number of mergers in industry is up by 20 per cent, with Community mergers growing by over 50 per cent and the number where the combined turnover exceeds 1,000 million ECU has grown by 40 per cent. Obviously the approach of the Single European Market has had an influence on corporate structures.

In some quarters 1992 has been used as the justification for the formation of new, very large, merged enterprises. Usually an acquisition has been promoted on the grounds of economies of scale. This is a valid concept, but sometimes I am concerned that emphasis on economies of scale overlooks other aspects of business to the detriment of a company's overall competitiveness. The 'economies-of-scale-by-acquisition' argument has less force than it used to. It is still relevant to some product markets, but not all of them. The case for new investment in new technology is stronger than ever, and nimble, flexible enterprises will frequently outperform lumbering competitors.

Let me make it clear, the Commission is not against mergers and acquisitions. We adopt a neutral attitude, and in fact view them favourably in many instances. For small and medium enterprises there are often considerable advantages to be gained from collaborative ventures, the exchange of ideas, the transfer of technology and formal mergers.

They are also one of the major means of removing inefficient management. What might be called the 'competition for corporate governance' can perform a key role in stimulating efficiency. The mergers that concern the Commission are those that insulate the resulting company from the forces of competition. Diversity and choice, the central elements of the

Single European Market, are achieved by firms vigorously and fairly competing against each other. Consequently, mergers which negate these conditions poison the very essence of the 1992 programme. This is why merger control is such an important matter for the future development of the Community's economy.

My duties are clear. I have to ensure that a merger or acquisition does not restrict competition, produce obstacles to market entry and damage the interests of consumers. In pursuance of these duties the Commission and its Competition Directorate-General must examine a relevant merger before it is consummated. To do otherwise would give rise to damaging uncertainty amongst customers, suppliers and shareholders. This pre-merger control is a key aspect of the new Community regulation which should be enacted very soon. It represents a new instrument which enhances and partially replaces our existing arsenal for competition policy. In this way it will provide a much needed coherence to this vital policy area.

The proposals for the new regulation establish a threshold of five billion ECU for an initial period. Any mergers where the combined worldwide turnover exceeds this figure will be examined by the Commission when each of the firms concerned has a Community turnover of 250 million ECU or more, unless all of the parties achieve two-thirds of their turnover in one and the same Member State. Otherwise, the matter will be dealt with by the appropriate national bodies. The thresholds will be reviewed in four years, and it is the intention of the Commission that they will be revised downwards after the initial phase of application.

The fundamental consideration in our decision on the proposed merger will be its effect on competition. If the merger is incompatible with this concept, it will be prohibited and if it supports the process of competition it will be allowed to proceed. In some cases the Commission will allow a merger only when certain conditions are satisfied.

The regulation on merger control embodies certain important principles. Firstly, it ensures 'one-stop-shopping'. It is clearly absurd to require the parties to obtain the separate agreement of several individual national competition authorities. With the new regulation the parties will normally only have to deal with the Commission.

In a small number of instances, the Commission may decide to refer a merger to a national authority. This will only happen where the state in question has informed the Commission that a merger is likely to create or strengthen a local dominant position in its territory, and the Commission accepts that this is the case and that the relevant market for the product in question really is the territory of that state.

The Commission has also acknowledged that Member States remain entitled to take appropriate measures to protect specified legitimate interests unrelated to competition (such as public security, plurality in the media and prudential rules).

Of course, the Commission competition policy is not limited to mergers and acquisitions alone: we have a responsibility to ensure a level playing field in the new Single Market created by 1992, and to apply the competition rules to all those areas specified by the Treaty.

Looking firstly at State aids, it has long been recognised that these are capable of distorting normal patterns of trade. In the context of the Single Market, they take on an added significance. As measures in the 1992 programme are progressively enacted, the opportunities for the more usual forms of cross-border protectionism are increasingly limited. In this situation, there is a distinct possibility that Member States will see State aids as a continuing instrument of protectionism, allowing them to sustain ailing local industries or to support national champions. If we are to make a success of the Single Market, this cannot be allowed to happen, and that is why the Commission is stepping up its efforts in this area.

A first survey on State aids, which was published last year, has been used to carry out a major review of policy on State aids, and I recently announced our future priorities. In particular, we have decided to concentrate more resources on scrutinizing existing aid schemes. Our aim is to assess whether aids which were granted some time ago, many of which received Commission approval at the time, are still justified on the basis of Article 92 of the Treaty. Market circumstances change, and subsidies which were merited at the outset may now be damaging to the Single Market and to our efforts to create a genuinely level playing field. We are now analysing the largest aid schemes in each Member State and I shall soon be putting to the Commission the first proposals resulting from this exercise. In the meantime, of course, we are continuing to look at new projects notified to us in the usual way.

Community competition rules are gradually being extended to two important sectors – air transport and telecommunications. In air transport, the initial partial liberalization of 1987 will be extended by much more comprehensive legislation. The restrictive agreements which have for so long dominated passenger air transport, to the detriment of the consumer, are on the way out. An open and competitive air transport system in Europe is essential for the Single Market, not simply because of the economic benefits – although these are important – but also because of what it means to the people of Europe.

In the field of telecommunications, where government controls have effectively prevented competition in the past, the Commission is pressing ahead with the programme set out in the Green Paper. The first Commission directives based on Article 90 of the EEC Treaty, aimed at liberalizing the terminal equipment market, has been notified to Member States; a second directive has been adopted, dealing with telecommunications services. These directives are designed to enforce existing Treaty rules, and the use of Article 90(3) is, in our view, the legitimate way of proceeding. Telecommunications services have an important and growing role to play in the Community economy. This is an area which is at the forefront of technology. It is also an area in which competition has been severely limited over the years. This is bad for business and individual customers alike, and that is why we are pressing ahead with our programme of liberalization.

The process of extending competition to services does not, of course, stop with these two sectors. There are clearly other areas which require our attention as we move towards the Single Market, such as energy, which we have begun to examine.

In addition, the Commission has been stripping away restrictions imposed by governments on purchases made by the public sector. Public procurement accounts for a substantial proportion of our GDP – somewhere in the region of 10 per cent. Only a small fraction of these orders goes to open competitive tender; the rest is allocated to favoured suppliers, often in the hope that this will foster some national champion. They are equivalent to 'no-go' areas on a level playing field. It is for these reasons that the Commission has been forcing the pace on the matter of public procurement.

The internal market is intended to bring about increased growth for the peoples and regions of our European Community by means of the process of competition. This book will undoubtedly contribute to a better understanding of the issues of competition policy as they apply in the European Community. Business cannot afford to ignore them.

Sir Leon Brittan
January 1990

Chapter 1

Introduction

The purpose of this book is to provide a broad and reasonably short guide for those in business and others who wish to become more knowledgeable about European Community competition rules and practice.

With the completion of the internal market in 1992 and the certainty that more mergers and cross-border agreements will result, a knowledge of competition laws will become increasingly necessary for those who have, or are contemplating, dealings with any other Community country.

The competition rules of the European Treaties have a constitutional character. One of the first articles of the Treaty of Rome states that the European Community shall include the institution of a system to ensure that competition is not distorted. Accordingly the European Commission has particular competence to implement competition laws and has the power to levy heavy fines on those who do not abide by them. Nonetheless, although the rules may appear to be very strict and the Commission's powers to apply them most significant, it is in no way an aim to be doctrinaire. It is a basic tenet of Commission policy that workable competition is the best stimulant of economic activity, since it guarantees the widest possible freedom of action to all. Consequently, the Commission is always ready to provide detailed information concerning European competition law and has always said: 'If you will come and talk to us, we can always give you guidance and generally find a solution'. Early discussion of a company's plans to make agreements, which might fall within the rules, is always to be recommended.

THE TREATY OF ROME

The Treaty establishing the European Community was signed in Rome in March 1957. The original six signatories were Belgium, France, West Germany, Italy, Luxembourg and the Netherlands. The Treaty was subsequently signed by the United Kingdom, Denmark and Eire to be effective from January 1973. Greece joined from January 1981 and Spain and Portugal from January 1986. In October 1990 East

Germany became unified with West Germany and hence it has also become applicable to the European Community Law.

Among the basic aims of the EC Treaty in creating a Common Market were the establishment of freedom of movement for goods, services, persons and capital between the Member States; continuous development and expansion of economic activities; an accelerated raising of the standards of living and closer relations between the Member States.

Over the years it became apparent that these aims were not being adequately attained. It was therefore decided that a date should be fixed in order to finalize the establishment of these and other objectives and also to achieve greater political co-operation, particularly in the sphere of foreign policy. Hence the Single European Act was signed in February 1986, ratified by all Member States and brought into force in 1987, with the aim of having a single market without internal frontiers by 31 December 1992.

Among the various activities of the Community set out in Article 3 of the Treaty was 'the institution of a system ensuring that competition in the Common Market is not distorted'. Competition, in so far as it concerns behaviour of undertakings or concerted practices, is then more specifically dealt with under Articles 85 and 86. Article 85 deals with agreements between parties which may affect trade between Member States through restricting or distorting competition within the Common Market. Article 86 gives effect to the prohibiting of abuse by one or more undertakings of a dominant position. We shall return to a consideration of these two basic Articles more fully in Chapter 3. The complete texts are also contained in Appendices 1 and 2.

Article 92 prohibits the grant to undertakings of any state aid which distorts or threatens to distort competition, in so far as such aid may affect trade between Member States. There are, however, some exceptions which are referred to in that Article. The handling of state aids by the Commission and by the Council are then referred to in Articles 93 and 94. We consider this subject in Chapter 8. The full text of these articles are contained in Appendix 4.

THE SCOPE OF COMPETITION LAWS

Broadly speaking, Community competition law has aimed to remove or to prevent barriers to trade brought about, for instance, by excessively restrictive agreements between undertakings, by monopolies or by various state subsidies. It also aims to encourage competition with a view to making the single market work to maximum effect by encouraging efficiency, innovation and lower prices.

Trading conditions between the countries of the Common Market have differed considerably. Some factors such as differences in taxes, excise duties, technical requirements, costs of labour and disparities in purchasing possibilities have contributed to this. Largely because of such different trading conditions, prices for the same products have frequently varied between Member States. For these reasons it has often been the case that manufacturers or suppliers of goods with higher costs and more expensive prices have tried to prevent or at least make it more difficult for purchasers in their own countries to buy the same goods from suppliers in countries where they are much cheaper.

Apart from these cases most agreements between undertakings of different Member States of the EEC have restrictions of one kind or another between them. These may often be perfectly justifiable but at times they are far too restrictive and effectively block competition. Among these are market sharing agreements in which parallel imports are prevented between companies in the same sector and which also involve supply quotas and price fixing. Furthermore, although Member States may be justified in helping smaller companies of their nationality, there has all too often been a tendency for them to provide protectionist measures for larger organizations, which either should not need much assistance or have only required it due to their being inefficient.

It follows that there are really two sides to the creation of a true internal market without barriers to trade. The one is the abolishing of the barriers themselves; the other is the ensuring that there is compliance with, and enforcement of, the European Community competition rules. It will be clear too that as the cold wind of real competition starts to blow through less efficient nations and businesses within those nations, the temptation for blocking competition from other countries will continue. State aids in particular will be likely to increase. Consequently it will be even more important for the Commission to maintain a full register of such aids and to ensure that illegal aids are dealt with expeditiously.

Chapter 2
The Community Institutions

Before proceeding to consider present EEC competition law in more detail, it should prove helpful to devote a short chapter to the four institutions of the Community. A basic understanding of how they are constituted, the powers and roles which each have appointed to them under the Treaty, and their methods of operation will facilitate a better comprehension of how Community competition policy works in practice.

THE COMMISSION

The Commission has three main responsibilities:

1. To act as the guardian of the Community Treaties;
2. To be the executive authority of the European Community;
3. To initiate Community policy.

Guardian of the Treaties

The Commission must see that the provisions of the Treaties and the decisions of the institutions are properly implemented. The Commission investigates a presumed infringement of the Treaty either on its own initiative or on the strength of complaints from governments, undertakings or private individuals. Once an infringement has been established the Commission asks the party in question to submit its comments within a specified period, generally two months. If the Member State allows the disputed practice to continue and is unable to satisfy the Commission, the Commission issues its reasoned opinion which the State must comply with before a given deadline. If it fails to do this, then the Commission can bring the case before the Court of Justice, whose judgement is then binding on both parties.

Executive authority

The Commission is provided by the Treaties with wide executive powers. These powers have been added to by the Council of Ministers to ensure implementation of legislation. Firstly, the Commission is enabled to enforce certain Treaty provisions and Council acts. Prime examples are in regard to the completion of the internal market and the implementation of common agricultural policy regulations. Secondly, the Commission is empowered to apply the Treaty to specific cases. In competition matters it must ensure that restrictive practices and market dominance are controlled and that limits are set to State subsidies. Thirdly, the Commission has to administer the safeguard clauses in the Treaties. Community legislation allows for waivers and exceptions and the Commission is responsible for administering these. Derogations are only granted when proven to be absolutely necessary.

The Commission also has the all-important executive responsibility of administering the Community's budget and the various funds connected to it. Furthermore, it has the task of carrying out international trade negotiations for the Community.

Initiator of Community policy

The Commission both commences the legislative process and ensures that Community policy is put into practice and forms a consistent whole. The Treaty of Rome lays down the framework and provides the guidelines for Community policy. It is the Commission which must put forward proposals for legislation within the outlines of the Treaty and must defend the Community interest.

The Commission is run by 17 Commissioners, each with a specific portfolio of responsibilities. They are appointed by Member States' governments and serve a four-year term. The present Commission took up office on 1 January 1989. The five largest Member States send two Commissioners, the other States one.

The Commission mainly works from Brussels. Each Commissioner has his or her own private staff who advise on the more political aspects of Community affairs and draft legislation.

The Commission operates through 23 Directorate-Generals known as DG I, DG II, DG III, etc. Each is headed by a Director-General, the senior civil servants of the Community. They have expert staffs working under them. They are responsible for drafting proposed legislation in consultation with officials from Member States, with national and

European trade associations and sometimes with companies which may be affected by the legislation. The Commission also has a Secretariat General and various services such as legal, statistical and translation.

Competition policy which is handled by DG IV, comes under the direction of the Commissioner for Competition. On 1 January 1989, this portfolio was taken over by Sir Leon Brittan who will hold the position for four years. The Director-General, at the time of writing, is Claus Dieta Ehleamann. He has working under him a multi-national staff divided up into five sections which deal with the following issues:

a) General competition policy and co-ordination.
b) Restrictive practices, abuse of dominant positions and other distortions of competition I. This covers electrical and electronic products, mechanical manufactured products and the textile, clothing and other manufacturing industries, distributive trades, banking and insurance, the media and other service industries.
c) Restrictive practices, abuse of dominant positions and other distortions of competition II. This covers non-ferrous metals, non-metallic mineral products, construction, timber, paper, glass and rubber industries; energy (other than coal), basic products of the chemicals industry; processed chemical products, agricultural products and foodstuffs.
d) Restrictive practices, abuse of dominant positions and other distortions of competition III. This covers steel and coal, transport and tourist industries, motor vehicles and other means of transport and associated mechanical manufactured products.
e) State aids.

European competition law is directly applicable in each of the Member States. Because of this not only the Commission but also national courts, and national cartel authorities with some qualifications, can be used to deal with restrictive practices.

The postal address of the Directorate General is:

Directorate-General for Competition
Commission of the European Communities
Rue de la Loi 200
1049 Brussels
(Tel: 32–2–235–1111 Telefax: 32–2–235–0128)

or

Commission of the European Communities
8 Storey's Gate
London SW1P 3AT
(Tel: 01–222 8122 Telefax: 01–222 0900 Telex: 23208)

THE COUNCIL OF MINISTERS

The Council is made up of representatives of the governments of the 12 Member States.

Although Foreign Ministers tend to have the widest responsibility and normally deal with the general business of the Council, each government sends to particular Council meetings that minister who is in charge of those matters under deliberation. For example, when foreign affairs are being discussed the Foreign Ministers will attend; when agricultural matters are in hand the Ministers of Agriculture are present; when internal market or competition matters are raised the Ministers of Industry, Trade or Economic Affairs, etc attend.

The Council is assisted by a Permanent Representatives Committee. This comprises the permanent representatives or ambassadors of the Member States to the Community. These are in turn assisted by a full staff who have responsibility for the various aspects of Community legislation. They are located in Brussels and are available and willing to help advise those of their nationality working in business.

Under the Treaty of Rome the Council has the responsibility to enact legislation put forward to it by the Commission. In 1987, the Commission laid 699 proposals and drafts before the Council. In the same year, the Council adopted 458 regulations, 40 directives and 125 decisions.

The Council can either adopt the Commission's proposal, in most cases now by majority, or it can change it by unanimity. Alternatively, it can delay the matter by failing to reach a decision at all. A dialogue takes place between the Commission and the Ministers in the Council who try to establish their national points of view. Mention needs to be made of the so called 'Luxembourg Compromise', first brought into being in 1966. This has allowed any Member State in the Council to invoke the veto for any piece of legislation which it has deemed to be against its national interest. The veto has proved to have had a profound effect on the subsequent development of the Community by bringing an increasing degree of paralysis to important aspects of Community decision making. The situation has now been improved by the signing of the Single Act. Under this a large proportion of all legislation connected with the creation of the single market is subject to a new decision-making process which excludes the use of the veto in the Council.

In 1974 the EEC Heads of State decided to meet regularly with their Foreign Ministers and the President of the Commission under the name of the European Council. The personal intervention of the heads of government has provided a forum for making major decisions or laying down guidelines in areas of importance. The Presidency of the Council of Ministers changes every six months and is taken up in alphabetical turn by each Member State. The Heads of State normally meet at the beginning and end of each Presidential term.

THE EUROPEAN PARLIAMENT

The European Parliament was first directly elected in June 1979. Elections take place every five years, so subsequent elections have taken place in June 1984 and June 1989. There are no national groups in the Parliament, only Community-level political groups. It has 518 members. The Commission is answerable to Parliament, which has the power to dismiss it *en bloc*. Throughout the year, except during August, the Parliament sits for one week in each month in plenary session in Strasbourg. Between the monthly sessions, two weeks are set aside for meetings of the 18 standing Parliamentary committees which take place in Brussels. The remaining week of the month is reserved for meetings of political groups which take place either in Brussels or national capitals.

The appropriate Member of the Commission or his or her representative, appears before the committees to give an account of the decisions taken by the Commission and to talk about legislative proposals which are being reported on and debated in committee. It is the responsibility of each committee to follow developments in its sphere of interest in detail, to examine reports and to put forward opinions and amendments to proposed legislation. Committees can also produce own-initiative resolutions. In the case of competition, the Commission writes an annual report which the Parliament's Committee on Economic, Monetary and Industrial Affairs considers. It has continued to express the wish that the Commission's annual reports should appear not later than the 30 April of the following year, but they do not normally appear until near the end of that year. Each year a rapporteur is appointed by the Committee to be responsible for examining the Commission's report in detail, writing comments for the Committee upon what the Commission has done or not done and leading a full discussion, usually in the presence of both the Commissioner in charge of competition and the Director-General. In 1988–9, the Parliament considered the Commission's reports on mergers and acquisitions, franchising and know-how.

The European Parliament also has the right to put oral or written questions to both the Commission and the Council. These can, of course, include questions on competition matters, and in the course of 1989 it submitted 162 of them to the Commission for written reply, while a further 54 questions were raised for oral reply. At plenary sessions of the European Parliament there is a regular question time for Commissioners who are present to answer oral questions. There is also a time put aside in each session for questions to the Council, when the President in office or the ministerial representative must provide answers.

THE COURT OF JUSTICE

The fourth institution of the Community plays no part in the legislative process but is vital for ensuring that the articles of the Treaty of Rome, and subsequent legislation, are properly and fairly adhered to. The Commission is entitled to bring cases against national member governments for infringements of the Treaty of Rome. Equally, governments have been able to bring actions against decisions of the Commission, as have undertakings and individuals also.

The Court of Justice consists of 13 judges. Each of these is appointed for six years, by agreement between national governments. The judges are assisted by six Advocate-Generals. The Court sits in Luxembourg.

Under Article 172 of the Treaty of Rome, the Court of

Justice has unlimited jurisdiction concerning decisions made by the Commission imposing penalties in respect of infringements of the rules of competition, and may cancel, reduce or increase them. Under Article 173 of the Treaty, an appeal may be made against a Commission decision on grounds of lack of competence, infringement of an essential procedural requirement, infringement of the Treaty or misuse of its powers. Among those who may bring proceedings are individuals, companies and Member States.

Under Article 177 of the Treaty, the Court has jurisdiction to give preliminary rulings on questions referred to them by national courts concerning, *inter alia*, the interpretation of the Treaty, since, for instance, those courts are sometimes uncertain about infringements under Articles 85 and 86. Decisions taken by the Court of Justice under these Articles are of considerable importance in ensuring that Community competition law is properly interpreted and correctly enforced.

Since the signing of the Treaty of Rome in March 1957 until the end of 1987, the Court has dealt with 3,011 cases: 1,672 of these were preliminary rulings, 561 were actions by the Commission, 119 were actions by governments, 21 were by institutions against another institution and 638 were actions by individuals. From then up to the end of 1990 there have been a further 38 cases dealt with by the Court, of which there have been 17 appeals against the Court and 21 preliminary rulings.

Chapter 3
The Basic Rules

ARTICLE 85 (1)

Article 85 (1) of the EEC Treaty defines the prohibitions in the rules on competition in very broad terms; namely, all agreements between undertakings, decisions by associations of undertakings and concerted practices which may affect trade between Member States and which have as their object or effect, the prevention, restriction or distortion of competition within the Common Market. It adds a few illustrations of what is considered to be undesirable, such as agreements to fix prices, limit or control production, share markets or sources of supply, or practices which apply dissimilar conditions to equivalent transactions with other parties. (The full text of Article 85 is reproduced in Appendix 1.)

The above examples are also typical of the types of practices which are prohibited or controlled under many national competition laws, yet frequently come to light during investigations by the European Commission, which often imposes heavy fines on the participants. Alleged infringements of Article 85 also come up periodically in cases before national courts and may be blocked, though in the Commission's view this does not happen sufficiently.

Apart from these illustrations, the broad definitions at the beginning of Article 85 (1) have provided the European Commission and the European Court, to which appeals can be made, with flexibility of interpretation to meet changing problems and circumstances. As a result there has often been uncertainty as to compliance with the rules. Over the years, the scope has, to some degree, been clarified by implementary regulations, decisions and policy statements by the Commission, by decisions of the Court (which has quite often reversed or amended those of the Commission) and by block exemptions for certain categories of agreements.

On several occasions the European Court has decided that there are various kinds of 'restrictions' which do not fall within Article 85 (1). Examples are where they are judged not to have an appreciable effect because of applying to companies which are not sufficiently important, or where the agreement is between companies which are not actual or potential competitors and there are unlikely to be adverse effects on third parties.

Companies which are and are not covered

An important factor is that Article 85 (1) has not applied to agreements between many companies which are small or medium-sized. This is spelt out in the Commission's Notice of Agreements of Minor Importance. The latest version was adopted in September 1986 (in replacement of the Notice of December 1977). (See Appendix 5.) This notice has considerably increased the number of companies that can benefit from exemption since combined annual turnover can now be up to 200 million ECU before Article 85 (1) applies. Previously the threshold was 50 million ECU (1 ECU = £.68). It should be noted, however, that if one undertaking owns more than half of the capital or business assets of other companies, or itself is more than half owned by another undertaking, then the combined turnovers are all included among the participating companies.

The scope of the notice has also been extended to services. Furthermore, although the market share of the participating firms must still not exceed 5 per cent, this is no longer calculated by reference to 'a substantial part of the Common Market', which, in practice, could be a single national market, but rather to the 'area within the Community in which the agreement has effect'. With the increasing integration of the Community into a single market this, according to the European Commission, will more frequently be the whole of the Community.

Apart from the fact that small and medium-sized companies do not need to notify their Agreements of Minor Importance or to worry about action being taken against them under Article 85 (1) with regard to these agreements, under that Article they can also be protected against being placed at a competitive disadvantage. This protection comes into force when a company attempts to grant worse conditions than granted by it to other trading parties for equivalent transactions, or requires acceptance of supplementary conditions which have no connection with the subject of the contract. In this case small and medium-sized companies can also obtain protection under Article 86 against large undertakings, considered to be dominant, which refuse to supply essential products or which sell particular products on the market at abnormally low prices in order to squeeze out small competitors.

Small and medium-sized companies may also be assisted by State aids (which are by no means always acceptable for larger companies, as will be illustrated later). Applications of the schemes in EEC countries in 1988 included the subsidizing of the cost of management consultancy services, assistance with investment, new technology development assistance, and the provision of low-interest loans.

Agreements and practices which are prohibited by Article 85 (1) must be between different undertakings. Where there is a substantial degree of control by a parent company over a subsidiary, the two will be regarded as a single undertaking. Therefore, for the purposes of Article 85, an agreement between them will not be regarded as restrictive, nor between subsidiaries of the same parent if those subsidiaries are all in a similar position. It does not, however, follow that if one member of a group infringes Article 85 (1), other members of the group are automatically regarded as party to the agreement or as participating in the infringement, although it may be possible that the parent company can be regarded as having influenced a subsidiary in this connection.

Agreements covered by Article 85 would normally be between companies of different Member States. However, an agreement between companies of the same country may also be covered by this Article. This can be the case even if the agreement does not apply to imports or exports. An example would be where a national cartel prevents or restricts companies of other Member States from marketing certain products in that country.

In 1989 the Commission took 13 decisions under Article 85(1). Of these, six were granted exemptions under Article 85(3), one was given a negative clearance, two were prohibition decisions accompanied by fines, but in another one of those a fine was not imposed, while there were three decisions rejecting complaints. 284 cases were settled because they were no longer in force, while 98 cases were considered by the Commission to be too slight to warrant further consideration. By the end of that year there were still 3,239 cases pending.

ARTICLE 85 (3)

Article 85 (3) provides the basic grounds for granting exemptions from the prohibitions of Article 85 (1). This is the case if any agreement, decision or concerted practice by associations contributes to improving the production or distribution of goods or to promoting technical or economic progress, while allowing consumers a fair share of the resulting benefit. The agreement must not, however, impose restrictions which are not indispensable for these objectives; nor must it give such undertakings the possibility of eliminating competition in respect of a substantial part of the products in question.

It is only the European Commission, and not national courts or national cartel authorities, which has the power to grant or to refuse an exemption and only if the agreement, decision or practice has been notified to the Commission for this purpose. On occasion, specified restrictions can be imposed on one of only two parties involved and need not be notified. An example would be where one party is restricted in the fixing of prices or business conditions for the resale of goods it has obtained from the other party.

These and other exceptions are referred to in Article 4 (2) of Regulation 17. This Regulation, which came into force in March 1962, enabled the application by the Commission of Articles 85 and 86. The text of this is to be found in Appendix 3.

It is by no means always clear how Article 85 (3) will be interpreted. If there are other justifiable grounds for granting an exemption, the parties are normally required to amend their agreement so as to fit into the provisions of the Article. When the Commission decides to grant an exemption under Article 85 (3) this is usually for a period of between six and ten years. It can, however, be renewed for ten or even 15 years, and may then be renewed again.

ARTICLE 86

Article 86 prohibits any abuse, by one or more undertakings, of a dominant position within the Common Market, or in a substantial part of it in so far as it may affect trade between Member States. The full text of Article 86 can be found in Appendix 2. The illustrations which the Article gives are similar to those in Article 85. In practice, however, the concept of abuse has been extended beyond those examples.

It took some time to decide on the meaning of the basic term 'dominant position'. Among the various explanations given by the Commission and the Court was one by the Court which said that it

> ... relates to a position of economic strength enjoyed by an undertaking which enables it to prevent effective competition being maintained on the relevant market by affording it the power to behave to an appreciable extent independently of its competitors, its customers and, ultimately, of consumers. In general, a dominant position derives from a combination of several factors which, taken separately, are not necessarily determinative.

There are more difficulties establishing what amounts to an abuse of a dominant position than in controlling restrictive practices and so, for many years, the Commission concentrated on Article 85; only in the early 1970s did it start to make use of Article 86. Since then there have been a number of cases which have been examined by the Commission, though they have been comparatively few compared with those examined under Article 85. They have almost always followed complaints made by undertakings to the Commission.

The decisions of the Commission have quite often led to appeals to the European Court, which has periodically modified those decisions or sometimes overruled them, mainly because it has not accepted the Commission's conclusion of what was the relevant market. For instance, problems have arisen in deciding on the types of products included in the relevant market.

Among those abuses of a dominant position found by the Commission have been: selling at too high a price or at excessively low prices in order to eliminate others; refusal to sell or to buy; discrimination in giving benefits according to nationality; the strengthening of a dominant position through a merger which reduced competition through the elimination of a competitor; tying customers, for example by the granting of fidelity rebates, this being a form of price concession which might even vary amongst customers buying the same quantities from the same dominant company, but depending on whether one of them had also bought supplies from a competitor of the dominant company.

Dominance within the Common Market may be held by a parent company together with controlled subsidiaries, even if the parent is outside the Community. Dominance may also occur collectively between several unrelated companies, especially in a concentrated industry, through parallel behaviour. It does not matter that the conduct in question takes place in a single Member State if it is considered to have had repercussions in other Member States. Article 86 does not provide for any exemptions to be granted or for any exceptions to its prohibitions, but it does not necessarily follow that an exploitation of a dominant position is regarded as abusive. Whereas in 1988 the Commission adopted six decisions under Article 86, of which three were decisions without fines and three, which were established as infringements, had fines imposed. In 1989 there were only two decisions, both resulting from complaints and they were rejected.

Chapter 4
Procedures and Enforcement

Organizations which are clearly aware that they cannot benefit either from the Notice of Agreements of Minor Importance or from any of the block exemptions available discussed below, should notify their agreements to the European Commission. They should also consider this if they are not sure whether their agreements fall within the prohibitions of Article 85 (1). In such a case, however, they can have informal discussions with Commission officials which certainly provide helpful advice as to what should be done or avoided. They might also be helped by keeping track of periodic notices published by the Commission on competition matters. These give general guidance on particular issues and indicate the Commission's views.

It should be made clear that businesses undertaking agreements have the responsibility of taking account of Articles 85 and 86 of the Treaty. If the parties do not cancel or sufficiently amend an agreement which falls within Article 85 (1) or fail to notify it, the restrictions and possibly the whole agreement will be void under Article 85 (2) and therefore unenforceable unless exempted under a block exemption regulation (see below) or by the Commission following notification. Such an agreement would also be ineligible for an Article 85 (3) exemption if its existence later came to light through the Commission's own initiative or through a complaint from another company. If the agreement turned out to be a serious infringement, heavy fines could be imposed.

Application can be made to the Commission for a 'negative clearance'. This means obtaining confirmation that the agreement is outside the scope of Article 85 (1). Once the Commission agrees that it is outside, then it will issue a written declaration that, on the basis of the facts known to it, there are no grounds for intervention on its part. If, however, the Commission does not accept that the agreement is outside Article 85 (1), then notwithstanding the notification, there is no protection given against fines issued on its part for the period prior to notification: nor would it prevent national proceedings from taking place. This means that in the event of the agreement being found to fall within Article 85 (1), it is certainly advisable to apply for an Article 85 (3) exemption, given that if this is granted formally, national proceedings may not be initiated or continued and fines are not imposed. The exemption is normally granted for between five and ten years but occasionally for twelve years and sometimes for fifteen years from the date of the decision. The exemption can also be renewed for a further period, which could be shorter or even longer. The Commission may revoke or amend its decision where there has been any change of facts which were basic to its decision, where the parties have abused any obligation attached to the decision, or where the exemption turns out to have been based on incorrect information supplied by the parties.

COMFORT LETTERS

The Commission has always taken a very long time to grant a formal negative clearance or exemption under Article 85 (3), the average period being two to three years, though it may sometimes be longer. Since this is unacceptable to business and since the Commission only makes a small number of formal exemptions each year, it prefers to send to the parties an informal letter known as a 'comfort letter'. This gives the Commission's view that it has no reason to intervene or that the agreement is exemptable but the Commission does not consider it necessary to pursue a formal procedure to a final decision. A 'comfort letter' will provide continued protection from fines, normally from the date of notification of the agreement. However, in contrast to the position in which a formal decision of negative clearance or exemption is granted, national courts may still apply the prohibitions under Article 85 (1) though they would in all likelihood take account of such a letter and so would not continue with the proceedings pending a determination by the Commission.

Before writing a comfort letter the Commission, in some cases, does the same as when it gives a negative clearance or a formal exemption; namely of publishing a notice in the Official Journal inviting comments from those who are interested in the agreement. Interested third parties having had that opportunity may be less likely to attack an agreement later on.

NOTIFICATION TO THE COMMISSION

In order to obtain a negative clearance, an Article 85 (3) exemption, or a corresponding comfort letter, a notification of an agreement, decision or practice has to be made to the Commission under the official Form A/B. Appendix 6 contains explanations of what has to be reported. If complete and accurate disclosure of the relevant arrangements is not made, either intentionally or owing to negligence, the result may be the agreement not remaining eligible for exemption or a fine being imposed under Article 15 (1) of Regulation 17 (Appendix 3).

Apart from what is submitted to it under Form A/B, the Commission has in any case wide powers to require undertakings to provide all necessary information. For this purpose, it may send them a written request with a copy to the relevant Member State, which may also be required to provide information. The request to the parties to the agreement must state the legal basis upon which it is made and the penalties for supplying incorrect information. If the information is incorrectly or misleadingly supplied, intentionally or negligently, fines of up to ECU 5000 can be imposed.

POWERS OF INVESTIGATION

When examining a particular agreement, whether or not it has been notified by the parties, the Commission may decide to send an inspector with its authorization to make an investigation at the offices of the parties involved. The inspector will usually be accompanied by a representative of the appropriate authority of the Member State. Inspectors have the power to demand that the company produces its books and records, provides extracts which are requested and answers questions. In recent years it has become more common for inspectors to turn up at company offices without prior notice. These 'dawn raids' have increased because of suspicion that with advance notice companies may dispose of many of their documents. Furthermore, the European Court has ruled that the Commission has almost unlimited powers of investigation when it suspects that companies have been forming illegal price-rigging cartels.

Various companies have, however, complained that they

were not sufficiently clear as to the precise purpose of an investigation nor whether the information being asked for was strictly relevant. As a consequence of this, the Commission started to be more precise and from late 1983 onwards began attaching to the inspection authorization an explanatory memorandum outlining the scope of its powers and the rights of the undertaking being inspected.

In the event of inspection taking place, the company may wish to wait for one of its own lawyers or an outside lawyer to be present before the inspection starts but the inspector may not be prepared to wait for long. It should be noted that correspondence between the company and an independent lawyer, which may be relevant to the inspection, can be protected. With an in-house lawyer there is no such protection, though in practice inspectors have not always insisted on seeing this correspondence.

If the Commission decides to continue the case, it sends to the parties a statement of objections with a description of the relevant facts, supporting evidence (if appropriate) and a statement of its legal conclusions. It may also ask the parties to produce pertinent documents.

The parties are allowed to see the Commission's file on the subject but not its internal working papers, nor secret matters received from other business firms who complained about the parties concerned which, if revealed, might have a detrimental effect on the complainants. The Commission may however give them a non-confidential summary of a confidential document. Furthermore, confidential matters may be disclosed when the Commission relies on the information as necessary evidence of an alleged infringement of the EEC competition rules. This can also apply in Court proceedings.

The parties may, if they wish, ask for an oral hearing before the Hearing Officer. This appointment was made in 1982 in response to frequent demands for the Commission to be more objective. The task of the Hearing Officer is to ensure that the hearing of the parties is properly conducted and to contribute to the objective of the subsequent decision made by the Commission. In this assessment the Officer will try to ensure that sufficient account is taken of all the relevant facts, whether favourable or unfavourable to the parties concerned, and that the rights of the defence are respected.

Before making this kind of decision, the Commission is also

required to obtain the views of the Advisory Committee which has members from the governments of each Member State.

The preparation of hearings has improved considerably over the years. The Hearing Officer, for example, may supply to the parties, in advance, a list of questions to be discussed, so that the key issues are dealt with more easily at the hearing.

FINES

If the agreement in question has not been notified to the Commission and it is concluded that the parties knew that they were infringing the Treaty or had not bothered to find out whether the agreement did (although they must have known that it was restricting competition), then the Commission will fine the parties. Fines have been imposed for many reasons and in particular for price fixing, market sharing, predatory pricing and export bans.

Price and quota-fixing and also market-sharing over a long period are, for example, infringements of Article 85 (1) and when, for instance, they were dealt with by the Commission in December 1988, the three companies involved were fined a total of 13,400,000 ECU. Yet, this was comparatively little compared with fines imposed in December 1990 by the Commission on two leading European producers of soda. For various violations of Articles 85 and 86, including their participation in an alleged cartel, one was fined 30 million ECU and the other 17 million.

Fines must not exceed 10 per cent of the total turnover in the previous business year of each of the companies participating in the infringement. Apart from the fines and prohibitions imposed on the parties involved, they may also, for instance, be required to cut their prices or to supply specific quantities of a product to a particular company, while joint companies may have to be broken up.

APPEALS

There have been many appeals to the European Court, pursuant to Article 173 of the EEC Treaty, against the Commission's decisions and/or the extent of its fines. As a result, on several occasions there have been amendments to the Commission's decisions. There have also been cancellations or reductions of its fines. This has not necessarily been because the Court has regarded the fines as too high, but sometimes because it has concluded that the Commission has got some of the facts wrong. The Court may increase the fines. In one particular case the Court concluded that while turnover can give an approximate indication of the size and economic powers of the undertakings concerned, the fine cannot be a simple calculation based on the total turnover – especially where the goods concerned account for only a small part of the figure. Among the factors which the Court has said must be taken into account in assessing the gravity of the infringement are the duration, the role played by each of the undertakings in the establishment of the restrictive practice, the profits which the parties made from it and the extent which infringements of this type impose on the objectives of the Community. The fact that the agreement is only for a brief period, that is for less than two years, can be a mitigating factor.

An appeal to the European Court must be submitted within two months of the Commission's decision. It may, however, take a long time before the Court starts dealing with the case and reaches its decision, since there has been a continuing increase in the total number of cases brought before it. Pending cases increased from 279 in 1980 to 395 in 1987. Of that total almost one-third of them involved staff cases and competition cases. The largest number of those, 77, were staff cases. These do not generally raise difficult problems and are in contrast to competition policy cases which often involve complex fact-finding as well as interpretation of law. The average duration of such appeals from the date of submission was nine months in 1975. By 1989 this had increased to two years. This growing increase has appeared to discourage appeals, for in 1988 there was only one judgment by the Court regarding an appeal by firms against a formal decision of the Commission. In 1989, however, there were 10 judgments delivered by the Court and in 1990 there were 15. Three of those in 1989 dealt with the Commission's powers of investigation and stipulated in particular that the Commission must clearly point out to the undertakings the presumptions which it intends to indicate. Many of the appeals in both those years (as indeed is frequently the case) were against Commission decisions, but they are almost always rejected, though in one case in 1990 the Commission's decision was not accepted and hence it had to repay the full cost, while in another case complaints by the Commission were dismissed.

A COURT OF FIRST INSTANCE

Even at an earlier stage when delays were rather less extensive, the European Court had found it necessary to propose that there should be another Court, which it referred to as the Court of First Instance. The European Commission and the European Parliament fully agreed with the need to have another Court. It was officially created by the Council of Ministers by a decision of 24 October 1988 and began to work at the end of 1989, with 12 judges. Since then it has coped with numbers of cases and its main effect has been to deal with appeals against Commission decisions on competition. In several cases it has rejected those appeals. After such rejections there can be appeals against it to the European Court, but only on points of law.

In one decision, in July 1990, the Court of First Instance held that an exemption under Article 85(3) does not prevent the application of Article 86, since it deals with different issues. It can also decide whether Article 86 can have effects on a given block exemption. By the end of 1991 it will also deal with many dumping cases.

COMPLAINTS TO THE COMMISSION

Enforcement of Articles 85 and 86 often result from complaints made to the European Commission. If these are well founded, they can obviously be helpful. The Commission has, however, expressed regret that it receives too many complaints from companies and individuals which have to be investigated and which turn out to be insufficiently justified. This wastes a lot of time. The Commission has therefore suggested that those who make complaints should first consider whether remedies could be available under national laws.

Complaints can be made to the Commission by those who have a 'legitimate interest'. This applies not only to third parties but also to persons who are a party to the agreement or practice which they fear might be contrary to Article 85. Third parties must show that they are, or could be, suffering injury or loss directly from the alleged infringement or, at least, that they have a significant and reasonably direct interest. Complaints can be made either orally or in writing. Wherever possible Form C should be used. This sets out the main particulars which should be given to start with.

NATIONAL COURTS

National courts may sometimes be uncertain as to infringements under Articles 85 and 86. They can always refer the issue to the European Court as a question of interpretation or validity of the Treaty. The European Court's reply does not, however, amount to a decision on factual issues.

Such references are made under Article 177 of the Treaty. The aim of this article is to help secure uniformity in the European Community in dealing with European legislation. It can be appreciated how very difficult it would be to create uniformity if Community laws were interpreted differently by national courts before which there was litigation. References have in fact frequently been made by national courts especially from British ones. In earlier years it used to take about six months to obtain an answer to requests for guidance. It may now take up to 18 months. This is unsatisfactory and has resulted in national courts being less inclined to approach the European Court and more prone to make their own decisions. The situation is, however, not as bad as it sounds since the national courts have available to them all the foregoing interpretations and decisions which have been made by the European Court.

Chapter 5
Block Exemptions

Since the enactment in 1962 of Regulation 17, under which Articles 85 and 86 are enforced, large numbers of agreements have been notified to the Commission to ensure that they are outside the scope of those Articles and, usually, also to seek an Article 85 (3) exemption in case the agreements are found to be covered by the prohibitions of Article 85 (1).

In general the Commission was taking several years to deal with notifications and produce formal decisions. These delays understandably became a discouraging feature for many organizations. Consequently the Commission began to appreciate that block exemptions were going to be necessary not only to reduce time but also to help increase the flow of trade within the Community. Nevertheless, the Commission has always been concerned about not allowing too many exemptions and this in turn has led, each time, to numerous criticisms on the grounds that the Commission was being too restrictive or insufficiently clear. This has brought about further drafts, criticisms and amendments. Thus for several of the block exemptions it has taken between five and ten years for these to be finalized, although by no means all the criticisms have, even then, been taken into account.

The first block exemption, covering exclusive dealing agreements, was by far the most common type of agreement notified to the Commission. It came into force in 1967, five years after the enactment of Regulation 17. Another five years passed before the next block exemption, on specialization, was enacted. Since then, both block exemptions have been revised, the first being eventually divided into two separate regulations dealing respectively with exclusive distribution agreements and exclusive purchasing agreements. They have been in force since July 1983, though they were not applicable to new agreements until January 1984.

Four other block exemptions came into force in the course of 1985. These dealt with patent licences, specialization agreements (replacing earlier revised versions), research and development agreements and motor vehicle distribution and servicing agreements. The main Sea Transport regulation relevant to competition came into force in July 1987 but a further block exemption was proposed in July 1990. The first two on air transport regulations appeared in January 1988, but since then several more have been enacted. Draft block exemptions on franchizing and on know-how were first made public in 1987 and the comments on them led to further drafts in 1988. The final version of the regulation on franchizing came into force on 1 February 1989, while that on know-how was finalized on 1 April 1989.

Many agreements fall within the scope of the block exemptions and need not, therefore, be notified. However, there are many others which still have to be notified often because of the various restrictions in the regulations as to what can benefit. Even if an agreement is exactly of the kind which falls within the scope of the research and development or of the specialization block exemptions, the firms involved would not automatically benefit if their combined market share exceeded 20 per cent of the relevant market, in which case the agreement would have to be notified to the Commission.

There are still some provisions in the block exemptions which leave uncertainty as to their scope. For this reason, therefore, several agreements have been notified for clarification as to whether they are covered by the block exemption or, if not, what amendments should be made for them to benefit from the exemption.

The Commission was aware of the further delays which these notifications could cause. It therefore decided from 1985 onwards to include what is known as an 'opposition procedure' for agreements which fall outside the scope of the block exemptions only to a limited extent. Under this procedure, unless the Commission opposes exemption of an agreement within six months of its notification, the agreement becomes automatically valid. These notifications have been used mostly in relation to the patent licensing block exemption (though often incorrectly, as indicated later – see page 53–4), but very little in relation to those on specialization and on research and development.

Because of all the notifications and queries either from companies, legal advisers or national courts relating to the interpretation and application of a block exemption, these exemptions have not saved the Commission as much time as it had hoped.

EXCLUSIVE DISTRIBUTION AGREEMENTS

A block exemption came into force on 1 July 1983. The Commission, in its 17th Report on Competition Policy dealing with the year 1987, stated that there were over 100,000 exclusive distribution agreements covered by block exemptions. Because of this, it had relatively little administrative work to do in dealing with such agreements. Nevertheless, it has still had to deal with notifications, queries and some usually unnecessary complaints.

A block exemption issued under exclusive distribution agreements applies to agreements made between two undertakings where one party agrees to supply only to the other certain goods for resale within the whole, or a defined area, of the Common Market. The second party may be bound to obtain the contract goods only from that supplier.

The preamble to the regulation recognizes the various advantages of such agreements, including the fact that it overcomes distribution difficulties more easily for suppliers, in that they have only to deal with one distributor who takes over sales promotion, customer services and the carrying of stocks. It may sometimes also be the only way in which the manufacturers, especially small and medium-sized undertakings, can enter into a particular market and compete with other manufacturers already present.

There are, however, various qualifications in the regulation. For instance, if end users can only obtain that type of goods in the contract territory from the exclusive distributor and there are no alternative sources, then the block exemption will not apply. In addition resellers in an exclusive distributor's contract territory can purchase the goods outside that territory from the same enterprise which is supplying the distributor. This, of course, could be to their advantage if those goods in that country were significantly cheaper. Not having to bear the financial and other burdens of exclusive distribution in promoting the product could enable them to undercut the supply enterprise's prices and so lessen its inducement to face those burdens. If, in consequence, the exclusive distributor were to find a way of preventing resellers from obtaining the goods from elsewhere, then the block exemption would not apply.

The block exemption would not apply either if manufacturers of identical goods, or goods which are considered by users to be equivalent, were to use each other or any undertaking directly connected with one of them as exclusive distributors so as to avoid parallel imports into each other's territories. For this they could be fined. A further stipulation is that even if an exclusive distribution arrangement between competitors is non-reciprocal, it cannot normally be accepted where both of the parties involved have an annual turnover which exceeds 100 million ECU. The exception to this would be where the turnover is no more than 10 per cent higher than that figure for any period of two consecutive financial years.

The regulation will not expire until 31 December 1997.

EXCLUSIVE PURCHASING AGREEMENTS

This block exemption was previously combined with that on exclusive distribution agreements and came into force on 1 July 1983. It will expire at the end of 1997. Exclusive purchasing agreements allowed under the block exemption are numerous – there being over 500,000 of them. The Commission also stated in its 17th Annual Report, that because of this regulation it has relatively little administrative work in dealing with these types of agreements.

Similarity of distribution and purchasing agreements

In certain respects, both the regulations on exclusive distribution and on purchasing agreements are very similar. The regulation on purchasing applies to agreements between two undertakings whereby the reseller agrees with the supplier to purchase certain goods exclusively from the supplier, or from a connected undertaking, or in the case of a reseller from another undertaking which the supplier has entrusted with the sale of his or her goods. The provisions regarding manufacturers of identical goods are also exactly the same.

Differences

The other grounds upon which the block exemption cannot be applicable are, however, different. In the case of an exclusive purchasing obligation, this must not be agreed for more than one type of goods where these are neither by their nature nor according to commercial usage connected with each other. Also an exemption will not apply if an exclusive purchasing agreement is concluded for a perod of more than five years. However, an indefinite period may be acceptable if the contract can be terminated within a relatively short period. For instance, the Commission has accepted a situation where the contracts can be terminated with six months' notice at the end of the first two-year period and, thereafter, at the end of each following year.

The other main difference between the two regulations is that the one covering purchasing also has provisions for agreements covering the supply of beer and the operation of service stations.

Beer

In this case the exemption would also apply where the reseller agrees to purchase certain beers and other specified drinks for resale on the premises, on an exclusive basis from the supplier or an undertaking directly connected with or entrusted by the supplier. This would be in return for special commercial or financial facilities. However, where the exclusive purchasing obligation relates to specified beers and other drinks as well, then the agreement must not last for more than five years. In the case of the agreement relating only to beers, then it may last for up to ten years.

Where a supplier owns the premises and lets them to the reseller, the ban on selling competing products is allowed to continue for the whole period during which the premises are occupied by the reseller. In this event, however, the agreement must give the reseller the right to obtain drinks other than beer from other undertakings which offer more favourable conditions or different trade marks which the main supplier cannot offer.

In June 1990 the Commission completed its review (which it had started in March 1989) on the block exemption covering exclusive purchasing agreements including arrangements between brewers and their outlets, and concluded that no general change was required.

Service stations

Similar conditions also apply in relation to the exclusive purchase by the reseller of certain petroleum-based motor vehicle fuels and possibly also other specified fuels. Here, too, the agreement must not be concluded for more than ten years unless the agreement relates to a service station which the supplier lets to the reseller or allows him to occupy on some basis.

PATENT LICENSING AGREEMENTS

The current regulation was finalized in July 1984 and came into force on 1 January 1985. Although there could have been several further improvements, many of the criticisms of earlier drafts were taken into account. On the whole, the regulation is regarded as helpful because it has greatly reduced the number of notifications of patent licence agreements. The Commission pointed out in its 15th Report on Competition Policy that prior to 1985 there had been around 100 new notifications each year. In 1985 itself there were only a dozen newly notified agreements. The Commission added that there were many more undertakings which did not notify but were able to adjust their licensing terms so as to take advantage of the block exemption.

What the regulation covers
The regulation concerns both patent licensing agreements and agreements which combine patent licensing and communication of 'know-how'. It appertains to agreements between not more than two parties. The agreement can impose various obligations. Among these are the following:

1. The licensor must not licence other undertakings to exploit the licensed invention in the licensed territory. This territory can cover the whole or part of the Common Market. Furthermore, the licensor must not exploit it there for personal gain as long as the licensed patent remains in force.
2. The licensee can be required not to exploit the licensed invention nor to manufacture or use it or the communicated 'know-how' in territories reserved for the licensor or other licensees. The licensee must not exploit it after termination of the agreement so long as the patent is still in force.
3. The licensee may also be required only to use the licensor's trade mark or presentation by which the licensor distinguishes the licensed product, although the licensee must not be prevented from being identified as its manufacturer. Indeed, the exemption of restrictions will only apply if the licensee personally manufactures the product or has it manufactured by a connected undertaking or by a sub-contractor.

4. Since patent licensing between members of the same Member State can affect trade between Member States, they are also included in the regulation.

Know-how

Know-how is defined as non-patented technical knowledge which is secret. It is now only covered by this regulation in so far as it permits a better exploitation of the licensed patents.

Conditions

Article 3 of the patent licence regulation contains a rather long 'black list' of conditions which are not allowed. Since some of these conditions are quite common in patent agreements, they may have discouraged numbers of patentees from granting licences. Among the various conditions not to be included or applied are the following:

1. Prohibitions on the licensee from challenging the validity of the licensed patent;
2. The automatic extension of an agreement beyond the expiry of the licensed patents;
3. Charging the licensee with royalties on products which are only partially patented, or which impose certain restrictions. These relate to restrictions on the quantity of licensed products which one of the parties may manufacture or sell, or on fixing of prices, or stipulating the customers whom the parties may serve, or which oblige the licensee to accept further licences which he does not want.

Opposition procedure

Patent licensing was the first of the block exemptions where the opposition procedure was applied. Under this, provisions which are not exempted by the regulation but which are also not covered by the 'black list' have to be notified to the Commission. These are regarded as valid if the Commission does not object to them within six months of their notification.

Notifications received

In its 16th Report covering 1986, the Commission stated that it had received 32 notifications under Article 4 of this regulation since it had come into force, but a number of these did not need to be, or should not have been, notified. For example, four of the notifications related to intra-group agreements and therefore did not fall within Article 85; four other cases did not concern valid patents, but know-how and trade marks; in six cases the agreements contained unacceptable provisions set out in the 'black list' of Article 3. Of the remainder there were only 12 cases the Commission decided not to oppose; that is, where they were considered to be agreements in line with the regulation.

In late 1987, there were four new notifications under Article 4, which were examined by the Commission in 1988. None of them was considered eligible for automatic exemption because two contained clauses referred to in the black list, and two included territorial restrictions which are not covered by parallel patents. In 1988 the Commission also dealt with five other cases, none of which was exempted under Article 4, although one was sent a comfort letter.

Advice

From the above it will be clear that businesses should carefully consider the basis upon which they are making notifications under the patent licence regulation and if in doubt they should consult the Commission before submission.

The Regulation will continue in force until 31 December 1994. It is certain, however, to be re-enacted since apart from anything else many patent licences last for 20 years.

SPECIALIZATION AGREEMENTS

The regulation on specialization was the second of the Commission's block exemptions. It first came into force in January 1973. It was extended and slightly amended five years later, was replaced by another amended version in January 1983 and was amended once again in March 1985. It is the intention that the regulation in its present form will continue until the end of 1997.

Reasons for allowing agreements

The Commission has looked upon specialization as being a contribution to improving the efficient production or distribution of goods. Where a manufacturer can concentrate on production of a limited number of certain products, there is a likelihood that these can be made more efficiently and at lower cost. Furthermore the supply of the products can often be made more cheaply and so provide benefits for consumers.

The Commission has therefore excluded the application of Article 85 (1) from agreements under which one party agrees not to manufacture certain products, but to leave this to the other party and vice-versa. Exclusion from Article 85 (1) can also take place where the parties agree to have the same product manufactured only jointly or by a third party.

The Commission may stipulate that the parties to the specialization agreements should grant to other companies the exclusive right to distribute the specialization products. Minimum standards of quality and a maintenance of minimum stocks can also be required from the party producing the products.

Qualifications

To benefit from the block exemption, the market share of the products which are the subject of the specialization must not exceed 20 per cent of the relevant market for such products. This includes other products of the parties which are regarded by users to be equivalent in view of their characteristics, price and intended use. In addition, the combined annual turnover of the parties participating must not exceed ECU 500m. However, as in other block exemptions, these amounts may be exceeded by up to 10 per cent for a period of not longer than two consecutive financial years.

In the case of turnover, the opposition procedure applies. So if the sales threshold exceeds the amount specified above, exemption will apply if express reference is made to Article 4 of the specialization agreement, full information is furnished and the Commission does not oppose it within a period of six months from the date of notification. The opposition procedure is not applicable in the case of market share where this exceeds 20 per cent. However, small but very specialized companies might have a larger market share than 20 per cent especially if they have an agreement with a big company which wants to benefit from their speciality.

Up until now there have been few opposition procedures with regard to turnover – only one in 1986, two in 1987, none in 1988 and one in 1989. No doubt there would have been more had there not been the market share restriction.

Withdrawal of benefits

There are two specified grounds which enable the Commission to withdraw the benefits of a block exemption. The first is if the agreement is not yielding significant results in terms of rationalization, or consumers are not receiving a fair share of the resulting benefit. However, these criteria may, in practice, be difficult to assess, depending on how they are interpreted. The second ground for withdrawal is if the products relating to the specialization agreement are not subject to effective competition from identical products or products considered by users to be equivalent in the Common Market. However, if the product was very specialized one might not expect much, if any, competition. It is to be hoped that the Commission will only withdraw the exemption in very exceptional cases.

RESEARCH AND DEVELOPMENT AGREEMENTS

A positive approach

The Commission has stated in the preamble to its regulation on research and development agreements, that both co-operation in this area and in the exploitation of the results achieved generally provide numbers of benefits. For instance, such agreements can promote technical and economic progress and can avoid duplication of similar work. Increased efficiency in the manufacture of the products or in the application of the processes often arises out of the research and development carried out. Consumers can also be expected at times to benefit from the introduction of new or improved products or services and from a reduction of prices resulting from the pooling of resources at the research stage.

Conditions

Joint research and development of products or processes and joint exploitation of the results both qualify for the block exemption provided that various conditions are applied. Firstly, the research and development must be carried out within the framework of a programme in which the objectives of the work are clearly defined as should be the field in which it is to be implemented. Secondly all the parties involved must have access to the results. If the agreement specifically provides only for joint research and development, without joint exploitation, each party is free to exploit the results independently.

Duration of agreements

Where the parties are not competing manufacturers of products capable of being improved or replaced by the contract products, the exemption will apply for the duration of the research and development programme. Where the results are jointly exploited, the agreement can last for a further five years from when the products are first put on the market within the EEC. However, this period can be again extended as long as the production of the contract products and any combined production of what users regard as equivalent products do not exceed 20 per cent of the total market for such products.

Competing manufacturers

Even if the parties are competitors the exemption will likewise apply, provided that when the agreement is entered into the combined production of the improved or replaced products does not exceed 20 per cent of the market for such products. The block exemption does not, however, cover joint commercialization of the research and development products by competitors. However, because of worldwide competition, there may be circumstances where an individual exemption may be granted.

Restrictions

The exemption will still apply even if specified restrictions, as set out in Article 4 of the regulation, are imposed on the parties by the agreement. For instance they may be obliged to communicate to each other any experience they may gain in exploiting the results, or to grant each other non-exclusive licences for inventions relating to improvements or new applications. They may also be required under Article 5 to communicate patented or non-patented technical knowledge necessary for carrying out the research and development. They can be required to preserve, even after the expiry of the agreement, the confidentiality of any know-how received or jointly developed under the programme. A number of other obligations may be imposed, including the payment of royalties or the rendering of services to other parties to compensate for unequal contributions to the joint research and development or unequal exploitation of its results.

Article 6 outlines those grounds under which the block exemption will not apply. For instance, the parties can be restricted as to the quantity of contract products they may manufacture or sell, the customers they may serve, or the determination of prices or discounts to third parties.

Opposition procedure

If an agreement does not fall within Article 6 but includes certain obligations which are not referred to as permissable, it must be notified. In that case, under Article 7, if the parties notify the agreement with additional non-black-listed restrictions and the Commission does not oppose within a period of six months then exemption will automatically be granted. There were, however, only five notifications for this purpose from when the regulation came into force in March 1985 until the end of 1987, none in 1988 and one in 1989, which was regarded as inapplicable.

Industry's view

There are some grounds on which the exemptions can be withdrawn should they come to light to the Commission. These are, however, either not sufficiently clear or realistic. There are also certain other provisions in the regulation which could have been expressed more clearly as to their implications and some which do not sufficiently cover research and development activities. The regulation has, however, been clarified in certain respects since it came into force and in general industry finds it helpful. The regulation is due to continue until 31 December 1997.

MOTOR VEHICLE DISTRIBUTION AND SERVICING AGREEMENTS

Before the final version of this block exemption came into force in July 1985, some 400 motor vehicle distribution agreements had been notified to the Commission. As there were also many complaints, the regulation and the adoption of its requirements had become very necessary. It has now clarified matters.

Special circumstances
It is understandable that suppliers in the motor trade wish to limit the resale of their motor vehicles to approved dealers. These dealers can be required to have technical expertise and to provide maintenance and repair facilities. They are also normally required to undertake sales promotion activities, to make sales and to place regular orders on the manufacturers.

Restrictions
In view of the above, the block exemption covers numerous restrictions between the parties. These include obligations on the motor dealer not to sell new vehicles of another manufacturer, nor spare parts which compete with the contract goods and which do not match their quality. The dealer is also required not to seek customers outside the contract territory, nor to entrust third parties with the distribution or servicing of the contract goods. It may also be necessary for the dealer to meet various minimum standards, to stock vehicles and spare parts and to sell at least certain quantities as determined by the supplier. Furthermore the dealer can be obliged to keep customers informed with regard to the use of non-original spare parts available.

Length and termination of agreements
The agreement must be for a period of at least five years. If it is for a stipulated period, each party must give a minimum of six months' prior notice if it does not wish to renew the agreement. Where the agreement is for an indefinite period, there must be at least one year's notice of termination.

Exclusion
The exemptions will not apply where both parties or their connected undertakings are motor vehicle manufacturers. They will also not apply where a minimum price is fixed for the contract goods. Among the grounds upon which the Commission may withdraw an exemption are when the contract goods are sold at excessively high prices or where over a considerable period the prices or conditions of supply for the contract goods differ substantially between Member States.

Many of the above practices existed prior to the aforesaid regulation and led to numerous complaints. Consumers and intermediaries also had grounds for dissatisfaction since it was made difficult for them to purchase the vehicles in the cheaper exporting country or to import, register and obtain free servicing or warranty claims in the importing country.

Commission action

The final version of the regulation became generally acceptable. Nonetheless the Commission still had to intervene in several cases where there was disregard of the Regulation. Some of these cases had to be put before the European Court for decision. Although complaints continued, the Commission would request manufacturers, importers or dealers concerned to take immediate action to rectify them. This had good effect and by 1987 the number of complaints had reduced considerably. In particular, suppliers moved to reduce extreme price differentations between countries and across their dealer networks. Consequently there was less incentive to buy a car abroad. However, according to the British Director-General of Fair Trading in his introduction to his annual report for 1988 (published in July 1989), there were still wide differences in prices between Member States and this remained until later in 1990 when the Commission was going to investigate the situation.

There were also other improvements. According to the Commission's 17th Report on Competition Policy, by the end of 1987 all European motor manufacturers had adapted the agreements which they or their subsidiaries had with dealers in the Member States, in accordance with the requirements of the block exemptions. The Commission had also received similar commitments from independent importers who were handling motor vehicle distribution in certain Member States. Consequently the Commission was able to close the files on the majority of the numerous notifications of motor trade distribution agreements made under Regulation 17.

In 1989 the Commission did not in any individual case have to take a decision to withdraw the exemption granted by the Regulation but it has continued to keep a careful eye on developments.

The present block exemption is due to continue until 30 June 1995.

SEA AND AIR TRANSPORT

The question of competition in the sectors of international air and sea transport had been raising problems over a long period. This was largely due to the fact that they have not been subject to Regulation 17, which is the tool for implementing Articles 85 and 86. However, the position has now changed once the European Court has decided, in a number of different cases, that the various modes of transport are, in fact, subject to the general rules of the EEC Treaty, including those on competition. Nonetheless, in the absence of a basic regulation, the powers of the European Commission were limited and it had, to a large extent, to rely on action being taken by Member States.

The need for regulations

Most of the principal airlines in Western Europe are state-owned. As such they have usually had the support of their Governments for various monopolistic practices, including long-standing pooling arrangements. As far as shipping is concerned, liner conferences, which are agreements between shipping lines having the object of rationalizing international services and stabilizing freight rates, have long been accepted in most countries as desirable in the interests of trade. The European Commission has also accepted the need to exempt liner conferences, but subject to limits and to control over possible abuses.

Nonetheless, it became increasingly clear that regulations were needed to cover both sea and air transport. Therefore, since 1979 the Commission made a series of proposals for such regulations, but, as always, it took a long time for them to be finalized. In December 1986, the Council of Ministers finally adopted four regulations in the maritime transport sector. One of these is particularly relevant to competition within the Common Market in that it lays down detailed rules for the application of Articles 85 and 86. It came into force in July 1987. Two regulations dealing with the air transport sector were enacted in 1987 and came into force in January 1988, while several more were developed later.

Sea transport

The sea transport regulation applies only to regular international services to or from one or more Community ports. It excludes the application of Article 85 (1) to agreements and decisions whose sole object and effect is to achieve technical improvements or co-operation in various specified ways. It also provides exemptions for agreements between one or more shipping lines whose objective is to fix rates and conditions of carriage, or the use of scheduled maritime transport services provided that they do not cause detriments to certain ports, transport users or carriers. Exemptions do not cover passenger transport or combined cargo and passenger transport, as the European Parliament had proposed, nor certain other of its suggestions. Exempted conference agreements may be monitored by the European Commission for any breach of obligations attached to the exemption or incompatibility with Article 85 (3). At the request of a Member State, company or individual the Commission may also withdraw a block exemption if the agreement has effects which are incompatible with Article 86. If an exemption is granted under the opposition procedure, it lasts for six years and can be renewed. Under the full procedure, the duration is fixed by the Commission's formal decision. The regulation also includes many of the same provisions which are in Regulation 17, including Commission requests for information from Member States or for them to make investigations. Likewise the Commission may itself investigate the books and records of companies. It must, however, hear the parties and third persons before making decisions and must also maintain professional secrecy. It may impose fines and publish decisions, but such decisions can always be revised by the European Court.

Among three other maritime transport regulations that also came into force in July 1987, one lays down procedures to be followed in response to unfair pricing practices by third-country shipowners engaged in international cargo lines shipping. Such practices cause serious disruption of the freight pattern on a particular route to, from or within the Community and cause, or threaten to cause, major injury to Community shipowners. Another regulation deals with co-ordinated action to safeguard free access to cargoes in ocean trades, and the third relates to the granting of financial support to transport infrastructure projects.

In December 1988 a further regulation was adopted. This laid down detailed requirements for the application of the competition rules to sea transport. In July 1990 another block exemption was proposed.

Air transport
The Commission had for many years hoped to finalize a regulation on airlines. Members of the European Parliament and consumer groups had also been pressing for cheaper air fares. However, most EEC governments and airlines were content to retain the status quo. The exceptions had been the UK and the Netherlands who were ready to make changes and considerably reduce air fares between their two countries, and later also with Belgium and Luxembourg.

The first regulations
The Council of Ministers eventually accepted the Commission regulations which both came into force on 1 January 1988. The first one laid down the procedure for the application of the rules on competition for international air transport between Community airports. Just as with the regulations for sea transport, this regulation sets out many of the same provisions which are included in Regulation 17 (Appendix 3). The second of these regulations enabled the Commission to grant block exemptions to various categories of agreements and concerted practice.

Other regulations
After approval by the Council in July 1988 the Commission adopted three block exemptions which came into force on 31 August 1988. Airlines were consulted separately and the public later. One of the regulations bore upon the application of Article 85(3) to joint venture agreements to develop and operate computer reservation systems for air transport. Another provided block exemptions for ground handling services at Community airports between suppliers of those services and airlines. This was dependent on there being no discrimination shown between air carriers and on allowing continued choice between companies offering these services. A further regulation dealt with agreements concerning joint planning and coordination of capacity, sharing of revenue and consultation on passenger tariffs in scheduled air services and slot allocation at airports. The provisions were intended to ensure that the agreements benefit air travellers, that airlines

can act independently and that agreements do not weaken the position of airlines which are not party to them.

Another regulation, adopted in December 1988, laid down detailed requirements for the application of the competition rules to air transport.

At a later stage the Council adopted a regulation on fares for scheduled air services which came into force in November 1990. Both Member States involved must approve a fare before its introduction, but the fare can only be disapproved if it is excessively high or low.

The three block exemptions referred to above expired on 31 January 1991 but were renewed on 1 February 1991 with several amendments on joint planning and co-ordination and also on the computer reservation systems. Those three regulations are to remain in force until the end of 1992.

In February 1991 the Council adopted another regulation, also proposed by the Commission, and which came into force on 8 April of that year. This established common minimum rules, applicable where passengers are denied access to an overbooked scheduled flight for which they have a valid ticket and a confirmed reservation departing from an airport in the territory of a Member State, irrespective of the State where the air carrier is established, the nationality of the passenger or the point of destination.

The passenger will have the choice either between reimbursement without penalty of the cost of the ticket for the part of the journey not made, or re-routeing to his final destination at the earliest opportunity or else re-routeing at a later date at the passenger's convenience. The passenger should also receive, free of charge, various expenses he had as a result of this, including telephone calls, meals and hotel accommodation.

FRANCHISING

The practice of franchising commenced in the United States in the 1960s. It only developed in the EEC in the past 14 years, but is now very popular and is continuing to grow rapidly. In April 1989, it accounted for about 10 per cent of the British retail market. The European Commission has generally approved of franchising agreements. Initially both the Commission and the European Court gave Article 85 (3) exemptions for a number of franchise agreements. It was then decided to produce a block exemption. The first draft appeared in 1987 and, following the usual criticisms and amendments, the final version was published in the Official Journal on 28 December 1988 and came into force on 1 February 1989. Under this regulation, a franchisor who is the owner of a trade mark, trade name, shop signs, utility models, designs, copyright, know-how or patent allows another, the franchisee, in exchange for direct or indirect financial consideration, to use any of those in order to market specified types of goods and/or to provide services. The franchisor may also under those conditions allow what is known as a master franchisee to make agreements with other franchisees. The goods which are the subject of the franchise may be manufactured by the franchisor or else on his or her behalf and will bear that name or trade mark. Since the regulation came into force, there have been numbers of notifications.

Obligations and restrictions

Among their obligations, the franchisors must provide commercial or technical information to the franchisee whilst the agreement lasts. Franchisees also have a considerable number of obligations, for example they must not, during the period of the agreement or for up to a year afterwards, sell or use goods which are competing with those of the franchisor and which are the subject of the franchise. The franchisees must not seek customers outside the contract territory. They must offer for sale a minimum range of goods and achieve a minimum turnover. They must carry out advertising of a kind which the franchisor will approve of. They must apply the franchisor's commercial methods and comply with standards of equipment and presentation of contract premises and means of transport. They must not disclose to third parties the know-how provided by the franchisor. The obligations regarding know-how, which is secret, substantial and identified may continue after the termination of the agreement.

The franchisee may also be required to let the franchisor know of any experience gained in the exploiting of the franchise and to grant it and the other franchisees a non-exclusive licence for the know-how resulting from that experience.

There are, however, several restrictions, listed in Article 5, which the franchisor may wish to impose on the franchisee, but which would not be granted exemptions. These include those which would restrict the franchisee from deciding the sale price for the goods or services which are the subject of the franchise. The franchisor can, however, be allowed to recommend sale prices.

Opposition procedure
As in some of the other block exemptions there is an opposition procedure. This is contained in Article 6. Under this, exemption is extended to agreements containing restrictions on competition which are not specifically covered by the regulation and are not prevented by Article 5, provided that the agreement has been notified to the Commission and the Commission does not oppose such exemption within a period of six months from the date of notification. A usual provision is that the exemption may be withdrawn in a particular case if the Commission finds that the agreement exempted by the regulation contains certain effects which are incompatible with Article 85 (3). In some of the cases examined in late 1989 and in 1990, the Commission found that the opposition procedure could not be properly requested since the agreements contained black-listed clauses.

Advantages
The regulation can certainly bring benefits to both parties. It enables the franchisor to avoid having to invest considerable capital in setting up a retail network with perhaps a large number of staff, and instead to achieve rapid growth and a broad geographical base by establishing a chain of franchises selling products of uniform quality and presentation. It can supervise and monitor the franchisee's way of carrying out the business which is the subject of the franchise, including its location, layout and decor. It may also limit the territory within which the franchisee may operate.

Franchisees obtain the benefit of being self-employed and independent, but without many of the normal hazards of establishing one's own business. If, as is often the case, they are at first inexperienced in the business involved, they acquire the benefits of the franchisor's expertise in relation to organization and operations and the training of staff. They may also have the advantage of having access to the franchisor's stock. Being a franchisee may also benefit a small independent company which might have been involved in the same kind of work for some time, but which has had considerable difficulty in competing for the same products with much larger organizations.

Franchising also helps to improve distribution and to assist the entry of new competitors into the market, especially small and medium-sized undertakings. It helps them to develop more rapidly and successfully than would have been the case without the franchisor's experience and assistance. They may also be better able to compete with large distribution undertakings.

Disadvantages

Certain disadvantages can of course arise. For instance, if the franchisee starts becoming successful he or she may begin to regard the franchisor as unnecessary and may resent the continuous supervising interest of the franchisor, so that a conflict of attitudes could develop. On the other hand, the franchisor may have difficulties if the franchisee is unsatisfactory, for while a poorly regarded employee can be transferred or even dismissed after due notice, it can be much harder to dispose of a franchisee.

KNOW-HOW

The European Commission has acknowledged the increasing importance of know-how. The large number of agreements being concluded by industry solely for the exploitation of such information, described as 'pure' know-how licensing, has been proof of this. Consequently it has recognized the need to provide greater legal certainty with regard to such agreements under competition rules. Although the block exemptions on patent licensing, on research and development and on franchising include some provisions on know-how, these have been by no means sufficient. The Commission, therefore, produced a first draft of a separate block exemption in August 1987. As usual, there were numerous comments submitted to the Commission and new drafts were produced. The final version of the regulation which came into force on 1 April 1989 has taken account of many of the previous criticisms.

In 1989 there were numbers of notifications on know-how arrangements and also mixed know-how and patent licensing. The Commission had to tell the undertakings concerned to bring their agreements into line with the conditions laid down in the regulation. Later that year there were other notifications which continued to be examined in 1990, some of which could not be automatically exempted either because they contained clauses included in the black list of Article 3 or did not comply with the conditions of Article 4.

Provisions of the regulation

The regulation defines know-how as 'a body of technical information that is secret, substantial and identified in any appropriate form'. It goes on to explain what is meant by those terms and other relevant aspects.

Article 1

This states that 'secret' is not limited to being totally unknown or unobtainable outside the licensor's business, but to being 'not generally known or easily accessible so that part of its value consists in the lead-time which the licensee gains when it is communicated to him'. The term 'substantial' is intended to exclude trivial information and to include that which is important for the whole or a significant part of a manufacturing process or a product or service, or for their development. This is so that it can reasonably be expected to improve the licensee's competitive position by helping him or her to enter a new market or giving an advantage in competition with other manufacturers or providers of services.

'Identified' means that the know-how is described or recorded in such a way as to verify that it fulfils the criteria of secrecy and substantiality, and to ensure that the licensee is not unduly restricted in the exploitation of own technology. As well as pure know-how, the regulaton also covers mixed know-how and patent licensing agreements in which the know-how is predominant, which are not, therefore, covered by the Patent Licensing Regulation, and where a technology containing both patented and non-patented lements in one or more Member States is licensed.

Among the exempted provisions between two parties which are specified in Article 1, are obligations on the licensor not to license other undertakings to exploit the licensed technology and not to exploit it personally in the licensed territory. There are also obligations on the licensee:

1. Not to exploit the licenced technology in territories reserved for the licensor;
2. Not to manufacture or use the licensed product or process in Common Market territories licensed to other licensees;
3. To limit production of the licensed product to the quantities required for manufacturing own products;
4. To sell the licensed product only as an integral or replacement part for own products.

The first Commission draft of the know-how block exemption regulation limited the period of exemption for most obligations for each licensed territory to seven years. This met with substantial criticism since it was in contrast to the exemption period of 20 years for patents. Also it was pointed out that there are numerous cases of know-how which remain secret for more than seven years. In consequence the period has now been extended to ten years. This, however, commences from the date of signature of the first licence agreement in the EEC and not, as had been urged, from the date on which the product was first marketed by the licensee. This may be much later than the signing of the contract.

The obligation on the licensee not to put the licensed product on the market in territories licensed to other licensees is still limited to five years. Previously, however, the obligation ran from the date when the product was first launched within the EEC. Now it is from the date of signature of the first license agreement, and so a shorter period.

Article 2

The regulation goes on to list in Article 2 a number of other exempted obligations which are commonly found in know-how licensing agreements, even though it is recognized in the Article that generally they are not restrictive of competition. These include obligations on the licensee, such as not to divulge the know-how or use it to construct facilities for third parties; not to grant sub-licences or to assign the licence; and not to exploit the know-how after the agreement has expired, so long as it is still secret. Furthermore, the licensee must communicate to the licensor any experience gained in exploiting the licensed technology and grant the licensor a non-exclusive licence in respect of improvements to, or new applications of, the technology. The licensee may also license these improvements to third parties provided prior approval is obtained from the licensor. The latter may not withhold such approval unless there are objectively justifiable reasons for believing that those licensing improvements to third parties will disclose the licensor's know-how. The licensee may also be obliged to mark the licensed product with the name of the licensor. Should the know-how become publicly known other than by action of the licensor, the licensee may be obliged to continue paying royalties until the end of the agreement. If the know-how becomes publicly known because of action by the licensee in breach of the agreement, damages may have to be paid in addition.

Article 3

There are a number of situations where the exemptions will not apply in view of various specified obligations or restrictions on the licensee, the licensor or both. These are referred to in Article 3. For example, if the licensee is required to grant the licensor an exclusive licence for improvements which would prevent the licensee from using own improvements, in so far as these are severable from the licensor's know-how; or if the licensee is obliged, when the agreement is made, to accept further licences or to procure goods or services which are not wanted.

Among other reasons for which exemption will also not apply are: if the licensee is prohibited from contesting the secrecy of the liensed know-how or from challenging the validity of any accompanying patents belonging to the licensor; if the licensee is charged royalties on goods or services which are not entirely or partially produced by means of the licensed technology; if a restriction is placed on the number of licensed products the licensee may manufacture or sell, or in the determination of their prices; or if the licensee is required to refuse, without any objectively justified reason, to meet demands for the products from users as resellers in their respective territories or else to make it difficult for them to obtain the products from other resellers within the EEC.

Article 4
Even if agreements are not covered by the exemptions of Articles 1 and 2 and provided that they do not involve the obligations or restrictions specified in Article 3, then according to Article 4 these agreements may still be exempted if they are notified to the European Commission and exemption is not opposed within a period of six months from the date of notification.

Withdrawal of benefits
There are a number of grounds which enable the Commission to withdraw the benefit of the regulation, some of these being similar to those in other block exemptions.

Non-Member countries
It is also intended that the regulation will cover know-how or licensing agreements for non-Member countries and for territories which extend beyond the frontiers of the Community if they have effects within the Common Market which may fall within the scope of Article 85 (1).

After coming into force on 1 April 1989, the regulation is intended to apply until 31 December 1999.

Chapter 6
Mergers

WHY A DIRECTIVE WAS NEEDED

The linking together of two or more companies into a single undertaking may sometimes help to increase competition, but there are also circumstances where a merger may distort both internal and cross-border trade. Britain, France and the Federal Republic of Germany had, under their national laws, been dealing with mergers over a long period, while many of the other Member States had seldom taken any action in this regard. Indeed, some of them had no existing merger controls.

National provisions can usually only deal with the domestic implications of a merger and rarely with its cross-frontier effects. Furthermore, mergers taking place between companies in two different Member States or having an effect in more than one State can be subject to different and sometimes incompatible national laws or practice. The European Commission became increasingly concerned about these factors and about the larger numbers of mergers either taking place or planned in the build-up to 1992. This was particularly the case where merging companies might create or increase a dominant position which could subsequently lead to a situation where actual or potential competition, in relation to the products involved, might largely be eliminated in a substantial part of the Common Market.

COMMISSION ACTION

Since there were circumstances where the problems which mergers raised could not be adequately dealt with under Articles 85 and 86 and also because of the differences or absences of national laws coping with them, the European Commission wanted to establish a more general measure to deal with mergers.

Consequently in 1973 it introduced a draft regulation on the control of concentrations between undertakings. This draft was strongly criticised both by industry and Member States and criticisms continued with regard to many of the numerous revisions.

However, the Commission remained determined to have agreements reached on a regulation. This was because of their firm view that it was becoming even more essential for a proper functioning of a single market free of internal frontiers.

By the end of 1987 all Member States had become, in principle, supporters of a regulation on mergers, though there were some reservations. More amendments continued to be made and the final version came into force on 21 September 1990.

THE SCOPE OF THE REGULATION

The Regulation is not intended to impede merger activity but to make it easier and to give clearance quickly; however, if it might damage competition it is also controlled quickly.

Under Article 1 of the Regulation, it will now apply to all concentrations having a Community dimension. This dimension has been defined as where the combined aggregate worldwide turnover of all the undertakings concerned in a merger is more than five thousand million ECU, and when the Community-wide turnover of at least two undertakings concerned is more than two hundred and fifty million ECU, unless each of those undertakings achieves more than two-thirds of its aggregate Community-wide turnover within a single Member State. Those particular figures will be reviewed before the end of four years starting from 21 September 1990.

Under Article 4, concentrations with a Community dimension must be notified to the Commission not later than one week after the conclusion of the agreement, or the announcement of the public bid, or the acquisition of a controlling interest. According to Article 7 the concentration must not be put into effect either before its notification or within the first three weeks following its notification. That period may, however, be extended by the Commission, though under Article 6(1) the Commission must examine the notification as soon as it is received. If it concludes that it does not fall within the scope of the Regulation, it will record that in a decision, while even if it is within that scope but is not regarded as causing serious doubts, it will declare that it is compatible with the Common Market.

If on the other hand the Commission decides that it does

raise serious doubts then it will initiate proceedings. It will also do so under Article 9, if it agrees with the concern expressed to it by a Member State that a particular merger may establish or strengthen a dominant position within its territory. Rather than dealing with the case itself, the Commission may instead allow the Member State to cope with it under its own national competition law. If, following such a complaint, the Commission does not consider that there is such a threat, it will adopt a decision to that effect. The decision referred to under Article 6(1) must be taken within one month, though if there has been a complaint from a Member State, it can increase it to six months.

If the Commission is dealing with the situation it may obtain all necessary information not only from the Government or the competent authorities of the Member States, but also from interested third parties and from one or more persons already controlling at least one undertaking or from one or more undertakings.

Officials of the Commission who will be carrying out the investigations in the countries concerned have to specify the subject matter and the purpose of the investigations and the penalties imposed if the required information and documents are incomplete. Officials of the Member State in the area concerned may be asked to assist the Commission officials.

It is now estimated that around 40 or 50 mergers will be notified each year to the Commission, which must then immediately publish the main contents of what has been reported. From when the Regulation came into force until the end of March 1991, there were 24 notifications of which there have been 15 clearances, three on which the Commission has opened full proceedings and two cases which were found not to be within the scope, all dealt with quickly by the Commission. There were four decisions still pending.

FINES, APPEALS AND CONSULTATION

The Commission is empowered to levy fines of between ECU 1,000 and 50,000 when parties intentionally or negligently supply incorrect or misleading information; when they fail to supply information within the time limit fixed by the Commission; or when they produce the required books or other business records in incomplete form. If the undertakings concerned intentionally or negligently breach one of the obligations imposed on them or carry out a merger contrary to the provisions of the regulation, they may be fined up to 10 per cent of their aggregate turnover. Penalties may also be imposed for each day of delay by the undertakings concerned in providing the complete and correct information requested by the Commission. Fines or periodic penalties imposed by the Commission may be reviewed by the European Court, which may cancel, reduce or increase them.

Under Article 18, the Commission must give the parties concerned the opportunity of making known their views at every stage of the procedure about the objections against them. However, a decision to continue the suspension of a merger or to grant a derogation from suspension of a merger may now be taken provisionally without the parties concerned being able to give their views beforehand, provided that the Commission gives them that opportunity as soon as possible after taking its decision. Where it regards it as necessary, the Commission or the competent authorities of the Member States may also enable third persons who can show that they have a sufficient interest to give their views about the concentrations.

Article 19 emphasizes that the Commission must carry out its procedures in close and constant liaison with the competent authorities of the Member States which will have the right to express their views on these procedures. Furthermore, an Advisory Committee consisting of one or two officials of each Member State must be consulted before the Commission makes its decision. This was regarded as important by the Commission, since it was concerned about Member States applying their own rules to the same merger between companies of their respective States, as this could lead to contradictory results and might not be favourable to the interests of the Community as a whole.

NATIONAL COMPETITION LAW

The position with regard to proceedings under national law against mergers has been clarified under Recitals (27) and (28) and Articles 9 and 21. Recital (27) states that Member States shall not apply their national legislation on competition to concentrations which have a Community dimension (as defined in Article 1) unless expressly empowered to do so by the Commission. Recital (28) and Article 21 adds that this principle does not prevent Member States from protecting their legitimate interests other than those to be taken into account under this regulation. However, such interests must be clearly defined and provided for in domestic law and measures taken must be compatible with the other provisions on Community law.

Mergers which fall outside the scope of application of the regulation can be dealt with by Member States. They and the Commission will not, as a matter of policy, apply Articles 85 and 86 to them.

Article 22 states that Regulation 17, applicable to most aspects of Community competition, shall not apply to concentrations falling within the scope of the mergers regulation.

UNDERTAKINGS OUTSIDE THE COMMUNITY

Under Article 24, Member States may inform the Commission of any general difficulties encountered by their undertakings in a non-member country. If in such a case that country does not grant treatment to Community undertakings comparable to that granted by the Community, the Commission may submit proposals to the Council for negotiations to ensure comparable treatment in that non-Member country.

STAFF

It was clear that for all the extra work needed to be done by DGIV in dealing with the Regulations, more staff was required. Hence a central merger control office has been set up. This is really another Directorate of DGIV.

Apart from officials within the Commission, there are also national officials on secondment from the Member States which are dealing with the Regulation. There are now about 45 altogether and they meet weekly to discuss cases and to ensure that consistent decisions are being made.

Chapter 7
Joint Ventures

Joint ventures are usually under the combined control of two or more separate parent companies. They often contribute to the economic objectives of the European Community. They may, for instance, be very useful in a field of research and development; when companies need the specialization of another or of each other; for the development of an important new product which would be too expensive for one company to produce; to facilitate undertaking risky investments; to develop a new market to reduce costs for the benefit of users; or to increase competition and in that role to help small and medium-sized firms which might otherwise not be able to penetrate a particular market. Joint ventures may be covered by the block exemptions on specialization or on research and development. In such instances, the European Commission has recognized that they can avoid duplication of the same kind of work and may help to rationalize the manufacture of the products involved.

Sometimes the object of a joint venture may be solely to share production facilities for certain goods with the participants maintaining their own brands and separate distribution networks and possibly remaining competitors. At other times the companies creating a joint venture may not have been active in that particular field before or, if they have been, may decide to withdraw from individual participation in favour of a joint activity.

A joint venture does not necessarily take the form of a joint company. Joint ventures which have been the subject of Commission decisions have included partnerships between economically independent companies and also a joint committee using the assets and personnel of the companies involved.

UNACCEPTABLE CASES

Joint ventures will often increase competition and economic growth and therefore be generally acceptable. On other occasions they can be regarded as anti-competitive by raising barriers which prevent others from entering the market;

through fixing prices and production quotas between the parent companies; or through excessive concentration of market power which can, on occasion, be taken solely because their combined market share exceeds 5 per cent. It does not, however, necessarily follow that because of these factors a joint venture will be prohibited. Much depends upon the merits of each case.

Where a joint venture does not fall within the scope of one of the block exemptions and is regarded as covered by Article 85 (1), an Article 85 (3) exemption may still be applied for. This would be granted in the case of the venture offering substantial economic benefits and not appreciably reducing competition in the relevant market. The Commission could, however, still require various amendments to be made in order to eliminate unacceptable aspects.

A QUESTIONNAIRE

The above various factors show that there can sometimes be uncertainty as to the position of a joint venture. For this reason the European Commission, in its 13th Annual Report for 1983, drafted a check list of questions which it can use with respect to each of the parties. These include asking whether the investment expenditure involved would substantially exceed the financing capacity of each party; whether it would be possible for each company to manufacture the product on its own and whether each could separately bear the technical and financial risks associated with the production operations of the joint venture. Another important concern under Article 85 (3) is whether the provisions of the agreement in subject matter, geographical scope or duration go beyond what is necessary for the setting up and operation of the joint venture.

PROMISED GUIDELINES

For these reasons the situation will clearly vary according to the companies involved and to particular conditions and circumstances. The European Commission has therefore acknowledged that a case-by-case analysis is always necessary. No separate block exemption for joint ventures is likely to be enacted. The Commission did, however, say that it would produce a notice involving guidelines on joint ventures, but for certain reasons this has been delayed.

In its 17th Annual Report for 1987, the Commission explained that the drafting of those guidelines was held up pending the enactment of the merger regulation because of the links which may exist between the assessment of certain joint ventures and mergers. The delay was also due to a pending judgment of the Court of Justice in a particular case involving some joint venture problems. Nonetheless, in 1987 and since then, the Commission has been making several important decisions on joint ventures. For instance, in a case which the Commission dealt with in 1977, it then granted an Article 85(3) exemption for 10 years to two parties of a joint venture and in 1987 it renewed it for a further 20 years. This was because it regarded the agreement as having continuing benefits and concluded that over the years the parties had become less restrictive and competition had remained strong.

In 1988 there were two more exemptions, one in 1989 and another one that year was given a comfort letter. In 1990 there were three exemptions while a fourth one was intended to be given a comfort letter in June 1991.

Chapter 8
State Aids

The countries which established the EEC were aware from the start of the problems which State aids might raise in affecting trade between Member States, through distorting or threatening to distort competition. Because of this, the Treaty of Rome contains three articles (92–94) dealing with State aids. These provide for their notification to the Commission which may decide that if a State aid is not compatible with the Common Market or if it has been misused, the Government in question may be required to abolish or alter it within a specified period. If that Government does not comply, the Commission or any other interested Member State may refer the matter to the Court of Justice.

It has been recognized that unless there is a clear and firm policy with regard to State aids, a system of free and undistorted competition cannot survive. Unfair State aids can frustrate free competition not only by preventing the most efficient allocation of resources but also by being used to the same effect as tariff barriers and other forms of protection. As the market integration process progresses and more and more artificial barriers to trade are swept away in the lead up to 1992, it is more important than ever that State aids should not be allowed to escalate as Member States seek ways to promote or protect their national companies in the face of increased competition.

However, it has always been understood that some State aids can be justifiable and necessary. Examples are:

1. Where help is provided for the least developed regions of the Community with particularly low standards of living and employment;
2. To assist areas where damage has been caused by natural disasters;
3. To help a particular industry which is going through a bad period;
4. To facilitate the development of certain economic activities or areas, provided that trading conditions are not affected to the extent of damaging the common interest;

5. To support research and development for new products and processes which may raise financial problems for the organizations involved, but which will be of value to the Common Market and may help increase competition.

PRINCIPLES FOR ALLOWING AID

Among the principles which the Commission has laid down for aid being given is that it must resolve problems rather than merely postpone inevitable decisions; that the degree of aid must be proportionate to the problem it is designed to resolve; and that unless aid is granted for short periods it must be reduced progressively and must be clearly limited to industrial restructuring. The Commission will evaluate State aids in relation to the general competition rules or to particular Community aid codes and policies for that sector or activity.

State aids take many forms such as subsidies, low interest loans, tax exemptions or reductions, indemnities against losses or the taking over of some company shares either directly or through public agencies. States may sometimes wrongly grant aids under headings which are regarded as being in line with stated Community policy, as, for instance, under the heading of innovation or high risk advanced technology, whereas the aids in question are really ones for general investment and modernization which firms should finance from their own resources.

State aids have frequently continued to be granted in order to help inefficient national undertakings to compete with more efficient companies from other Member States. Whilst these aids may prevent such national undertakings from collapse, they may also create industrial problems and unemployment in the other Community countries. Furthermore, such aids can distort competition and so can seriously prejudice the aims of a single unified market.

REGISTER OF STATE AIDS

The Directorate-General of Competition has always had to spend considerable time examining the large number of State aids which have continued to exist and a big section of its annual report deals with these cases. It has now completed a comprehensive list of State aids in all member countries and has expressed its determination to ensure that this is kept fully up to date.

It has been found that, on average, State aids represent 3 per cent of gross domestic product (GDP), but in certain Member States they are over 5 per cent. In the manufacturing branch, the aid given in the EC has been, on average, equivalent to a grant of ECU 2000 per employee. Since aids are not evenly spread out over all the sectors which make up manufacturing, certain sources have been receiving considerably more than this. In has also been established that State aids are around 10 per cent of public expenditure but in one Member State amounted to 19 per cent. Furthermore aids exceeded the revenue generated from the direct taxation of companies, as was stated in the Commission's *First Survey of State Aids in the European Community* published in 1989. As subsequently mentioned in a speech by Sir Leon Brittan, the total annual volume of State aid in 1988 amounted to one hundred billion ECU. In most Member States around half the aid was given to railways (23 billion ECU), coal (12 billion ECU), and agriculture (10 billion ECU). A further 23 billion ECU was given to agriculture and fisheries by direct Community intervention.

Clearly, with the magnitude of present aid given and the risk of new aid materializing, there became a growing need for the Commission to maintain a fully up-to-date register of State aids and to have the resources and support for forcing a reduction in those aids which are hindering the development of open competition throughout the Community. The diversification of the forms of aid will also make it necessary for the Commission to establish both the mechanisms and the instruments for each country to enable proper comparison and effective action to take place.

It is clearly important that Member States should be able to compete on equal terms in the Common Market and it is one of the Commission's main tasks to see that they do so. Some countries have by no means always notified the aids they have granted and have often concealed them by complex measures. It is invidious that some Member States have been found to provide aid to their own industries, but at the same time to have strongly objected to such aids being granted by other Member States declaring them to be prejudicial to their own national interests.

Because of the aids which had not been reported but which nevertheless came to light, the Commission decided towards the end of 1985 that there should be repayment of aids granted illegally. The Commission was therefore asked to provide more information as to what exactly should be reported; what types of aid would be acceptable; and what procedures and decisions the Commission has eventually taken.

In 1989 there were approximately 471 proposals notified to the Commission and there were no objections to 378 of those, while the rest were either regarded as incompatible and were prohibited by the Commission or else were withdrawn by the Member States themselves. There were eight decisions in which the Commission required the repayment of aid granted unlawfully.

In 1990 there were fewer notifications than in 1989, but numbers of similar decisions by the Commission. There were also several appeals against the Commission to the European Court, which normally rejects them. There was, however, a very unusual case where the European Court overturned a decision by the Commission, finding that it had made some errors of judgment in its assessment of the facts.

Chapter 9
Anti-Dumping

WHAT IS DUMPING?

There have been a number of general regulations in the Common Market to protect Community organizations against dumped or subsidized imports from non-EEC countries. These also applied in relation to new Member States during the transitional period of their entry, with a modified procedure. The main current regulation came into force in July 1984. There was also another regulation in July 1984, for coal and steel products, but in both respects the two regulations were similar. A revised main draft text appeared in August 1990, but that contained various alternatives for views to be taken. A temporary one came into force in late November of that year but was only intended to continue until the end of May 1991. Since the beginning of 1991 four other dumping regulations on different imports have come into force, originating from China, Japan and the US.

Dumping is generally regarded to take place where the export price of a product is less than the normal price for the same product in the exporting country or the country of origin. There are, however, various factors which the Commission takes into account in relation to the basis of these prices and before coming to any decision.

Investigations by the Commission normally arise out of complaints rather than through its own initiative. The complainants must show that they represent the majority of the Community industry which produces the same product; they should also be able to show that the effect of the dumped or subsidized imports has been causing them substantial injury. Furthermore, the prices used for comparison must normally cover a period of not less than six months or even twelve months before proceedings are initiated by the Commission.

Account must also be taken of prices varying considerably between different countries, since the labour costs in the country from where the goods originate may be much lower, or else the production may be more modernized or efficient.

Also, an exporter from another country may consider it necessary to make his prices lower than in his own country so as to compete more effectively with equivalent products exported from cheaper producing countries. An exporter may also be obliged to sustain temporarily lower prices in order to be able to enter the market to which he is starting to export.

The product which is sold abroad may differ slightly from that sold in the producer's own country and may possibly be cheaper to produce. Prices may also differ because of the greater quantities which are sold abroad. There may also be heavier taxes in the home country which could cause retail prices to be higher than in export markets where the taxes are lower. There may also be cases where the producer may obtain very good prices in his own country but may still be able to sell the same goods at cheaper prices abroad without incurring a loss, even though exports involve various extra costs. These are among the many factors which the Commission takes into account in deciding whether import prices in the Community amount to dumping.

PROCEDURE FOR COMPLAINANTS

For those who believe that they have grounds for complaint, it may be helpful first to seek the Commission's view as to whether the complaint is likely to call for the Commission's intervention and thereby a decision that it amounts to dumping and injury in the Community. Any complaints which the Commission receives are first sent to the Member States and in any instance when it decides to continue with anti-dumping procedures, it consults the Advisory Committee which includes representatives of each Member State.

Complaints can also be submitted through the Member State of the complainant rather than directly to the Commission. If the Member State takes the view that the evidence is insufficient and yet believes that the complaint should be forwarded to the Commission, it may add some additional evidence of its own. Even if there has been no complaint but the Member State has sufficient information of dumping or subsidies with resulting injury for the Community industry, then it must give such evidence to the Commission.

Should complaints later be withdrawn, the Commission

may nevertheless continue the proceedings if it believes that Community interests require this. If it concludes that there is sufficient evidence to justify initiating a proceeding, it will announce it in the Official Journal, indicating the product and countries involved, giving a summary of the evidence it has received and inviting information which can be submitted to it within a specified period.

The Commission may then request Member States to supply information and to carry out necessary checks. It will hear interested parties and will also, on request, give the parties directly concerned an opportunity to meet so that their respective views may be presented, though there is no obligation to attend such a meeting.

The information which is provided will normally be regarded as confidential. The Commission can also make investigations regarding faulty goods in the countries of manufacture. This will, however, be subject to the manufacturer and the Government in question being notified and raising no objection.

If it becomes apparent after consultation that protective measures are unnecessary, then provided that the Advisory Committee does not object, the proceedings will be ended and the Commission will announce the termination in its Official Journal. In all other cases, it will submit a report to the Council on the results of its investigations.

If the Commission does conclude that there has been dumping, its objective is normally to restore normal competitive conditions rather than to punish the company causing the dumping. In the course of the investigation, the company involved may offer an undertaking either to raise the price or to reduce the quantities exported. Where a subsidy has been received, it may arrange to have it eliminated or limited. Undertakings have to be offered within a specified period; otherwise the Commission will continue with the proceedings.

Where a preliminary examination shows that there has been either dumping or a subsidy, the Commission, either on its own initiative or at the request of a Member State, will, as indicated earlier, impose a provisional anti-dumping duty or, in the case of subsidies, a countervailing duty to offset it. In such cases, free circulation of products will be conditional on the providing of security for the amount of the provisional duty. Once the dumping or subsidy and the resultant injury have been finally established, definite action is then taken by the Council of Ministers.

At least one year after the conclusion of an investigation, the anti-dumping duty may be reviewed at the request of interested parties, at the initiation of the Commission, or at the request of a Member State. In any case, the dumping duties and undertakings lapse after five years from the date when they came into force or were modified. Within six months prior to that date, the Commission normally publishes a notice in the Official Journal so that the Community industry which is concerned can make known their views if they want to. If they can prove that the expiry of the measure would lead to an injury or threat of injury, the Commission may review the measure. Once the period lapses the Commission publishes a notice to that effect in the Official Journal.

An anti-dumping duty may also be imposed on similar products which are assembled in the EEC by a party which is related to, or associated with, a manufacturer from a non-Member country whose exports have been made subject to a definite anti-dumping duty. This is also the case when the EEC assembly or production operation is started, or substantially increased, after the anti-dumping investigation has led to that duty being imposed. However, in the latter case, at least 60 per cent of all parts and materials used must come from the non-Member country exporting the product; in other words their value must exceed by at least 50 per cent the value of all other parts or materials used. By the subsequent investigation, the Commission of course takes into account the costs incurred in the assembly or production operation, research and development and technology applied within the EEC. Those who assemble or produce the products must declare them to the customs authorities before marketing them in the Common Market. Duty would not apply if the products are then to be exported outside the EEC.

Chapter 10

Competition and the Single Market

1992: THE SINGLE MARKET

It is appropriate to complete this short book with reference to the completion of the single market by 1992, and the effects that this will have on competition.

The founding Members of the European Community set out to create a Common Market in which there would be freedom of trade and open competition between all the Member States. The all too common barriers to trade and other forms of protectionism were to be removed in order to bring about a greater incentive for doing business between one State and another.

In practice, trading conditions in the Member States have continued to differ considerably and monopolistic practices, varying national standards and customs barriers have, amongst other reasons, resulted in the Community being unable to make full use of its strength as a single market. Consequently, both the United States and Japan have made headway against the nations of the EEC.

It is true that over the years many improvements were made to remove barriers for a greater freedom of movement of people, goods, services and capital. However, the process has not been nearly fast enough and the increase in the number of Member States from six during the first 16 years of the Community's existence to 12 by 1986, has added to the complexities. The Heads of State of the Community therefore decided after pressure from industry, from the European Parliament and from the Commission, to set up a committee to study the advantages and methods of implementing a programme for the removal of trade barriers for the general benefit of the 320 million inhabitants of the Community and to make industry more competitive. The committee's recommendations led to the drafting and passing of the Single European Act which was ratified by all Member States in 1986 and brought into force in 1987. This Act had, as a prime objective, the creation of a single market by 31 December 1992 and incorporated measures which enabled the Commission to bring forward 279 separate pieces of legislation to achieve this end. The Act also gave the European Parliament amended powers to propose legislation under the programme and abolished the veto of the Council of Ministers on almost all measures connected with the 1992 programme, with the exception of those relating to taxation.

On the following page is a diagram which shows the main barriers being attacked and those sectors in industry and services which are most affected.

The removal of the remaining barriers to trade within the EEC will increase the ease and incentive for greater trading between the countries of the Community and hence for increasing competition, employment and wealth. Economic benefits are particularly expected to accrue from this, with most of the other savings coming from the removal of product restraints and from economies of scale. It has been estimated that the possible savings to be achieved will amount to 265 billion ECU or an equivalent of US $280 billion. More favourable conditions for producers should lead to better conditions for consumers. Banking, investment services and insurance are now coming under scrutiny in order to widen consumer choice and to reduce and eliminate local protectionism.

COMPETITIVE PRESSURES

With regard to the competitive sphere, and since the Single European Act was signed, the European Commission has made a number of changes to help clarify the position as to notification of agreements between companies. It recognizes that such agreements will certainly increase with the completion of the internal market. Thus, under the revised Notice of Agreements of Minor Importance which was adopted in September 1986, the Commission has considerably increased the number of companies which are exempt from having to notify their agreements to the Commission. The threshold has been raised from a combined annual turnover of 50 million ECU to one of 200 million ECU.

The Commission has also increased the number of block exemptions, which has helped many organizations to decide whether or not they should notify their agreements to the Commission. At the time of writing the block exemption on mergers had, however, still to be finalized after a great many years since the first draft originally appeared. As the coming

	Customs & Import Controls	Public Procurement	Taxes	Technical Standards	Health, Safety & Environment	National Monopoly	Government Licensing	State Aids
INDUSTRY								
Aerospace		●		○		▲		▲
Automotive	●		●	●	●			▲
Engineering	○	▲	○	●	●			
Construction	○	●		●	●			
Chemicals		○			●			
Food & drink	▲		▲	●	●			
Telecommunications equipment	○	●		●		●		
Consumer electronics	▲		○	●	▲			
Domestic appliances	▲		○	●	●			
Pharmaceuticals	○	●	▲		●			
SERVICES								
Air transport	▲		▲			●	●	○
Banking	▲		▲				●	
Electricity		▲			▲	●		▲
Insurance	▲						●	
Telecommunications		▲		●		●		
Road transport	●		●	▲	●		●	

The main barriers and sectors affected by the completion of a single European market

● *High* ▲ *Medium* ○ *Low*

into force of the single market has led and will continue to lead to a growing number of mergers and takeovers in order to increase market share and market spread, there is an even greater need for a mergers directive to reach the statute-book. The question of mergers and acquisitions, particularly amongst larger companies, is not always an open and shut case for the better since competition may be hindered in the process. The Commission will therefore have the task of analysing whether, in its view, greater concentration will lead to lower costs and greater efficiency or to an excessive growth of monopolies.

With the completion of the internal market in 1992, enhanced competition between Member States may lead to greater pressure from industries within those States to get an increase in State aid from their own governments. Quite clearly, such increases must be avoided if the 1992 programme and its beneficial results are to achieve their goals.

APPENDIX I

EEC Treaty: Competition

ARTICLE 85

1. The following shall be prohibited as incompatible with the common market: all agreements between undertakings, decisions by associations of undertakings and concerted practices which may affect trade between Member States and which have as their object or effect the prevention restriction or distortion of competition within the common market, and in particular those which:

(a) directly or indirectly fix purchase or selling prices or any other trading conditions;

(b) limit or control production, markets, technical development, or investment;

(c) share markets or sources of supply;

(d) apply dissimilar conditions to equivalent transactions with other trading parties, thereby placing them at a competitive disadvantage;

(e) make the conclusion of contracts subject to acceptance by the other parties of supplementary obligations which, by their nature or according to commercial usage, have no connection with the subject of such contracts.

2. Any agreements or decisions prohibited pursuant to this Article shall be automatically void.

3. The provisions of paragraph 1 may, however, be declared inapplicable in the case of;

— any agreement or category of agreements between undertakings;

— any decision or category of decisions by associations of undertakings;

— any concerted practice or category of concerted practices;

which contributes to improving the production or distribution of goods or to promoting technical or economic progress, while allowing consumers a fair share of the resulting benefit, and which does not:

(a) impose on the undertakings concerned restrictions which are not indispensable to the attainment of these objectives;

(b) afford such undertakings the possibility of eliminating competition in respect of a substantial part of the products in question.

APPENDIX II

EEC Treaty: Competition

ARTICLE 86

Any abuse by one or more undertakings of a dominant position within the common market or in a substantial part of it shall be prohibited as incompatible with the common market in so far as it may affect trade between Member States. Such abuse may, in particular, consist in:

(a) directly or indirectly imposing unfair purchase or selling prices or unfair trading conditions;

(b) limiting production, markets or technical development to the prejudice of consumers;

(c) applying dissimilar conditions to equivalent transactions with other trading parties, thereby placing them at a competitive disadvantage;

(d) making the conclusion of contracts subject to acceptance by the other parties of supplementary obligations which, by their nature or according to commercial usage, have no connection with the subject of such contracts.

APPENDIX III

Regulation 17

THE COUNCIL OF EUROPEAN ECONOMIC COMMUNITY

Having regard to the Treaty establishing the European Economic Community, and in particular Article 87 thereof;

Having regard to the proposal from the Commission;

Having regard to the Opinion of the Economic and Social Committee;

Having regard to the Opinion of the European Parliament;

Whereas, in order to establish a system ensuring that competition shall not be distorted in the common market, it is necessary to provide for balanced application of Articles 85 and 86 in a uniform manner in the Member States;

Whereas in establishing the rules for applying Article 85(3) account must be taken of the need to ensure effective supervision and to simplify administration to the greatest possible extent;

Whereas it is accordingly necessary to make it obligatory, as a general principle, for undertakings which seek application of Article 85(3) to notify to the Commission their agreements, decisions and concerted practices;

Whereas on the one hand, such agreements, decisions and concerted practices are probably very numerous and cannot therefore all be examined at the same time and, on the other hand, some of them have special features which may make them less prejudicial to the development of the common market;

Whereas there is consequently a need to make more flexible arrangements for the time being in respect of certain categories of agreement, decision and concerted practice without prejudicing their validity under Article 85;

Whereas it may be in the interest of undertakings to know whether any agreements, decisions or practices to which they are party, or propose to become party, may lead to action on the part of the Commission pursuant to Article 85(1) or Article 86;

Whereas, in order to secure uniform application of Articles 85 and 86 in the common market, rules must be made under which the Commission, acting in close and constant liaison with the competent authorities of the Member States, may take the requisite measures for applying those Articles;

Whereas for this purpose the Commission must have the co-operation of the competent authorities of the Member States and be empowered, throughout the common market, to require such information to be supplied and to undertake such investigations as are necessary to bring to light any agreement, decision or concerted practice prohibited by Article 85(1) or any abuse of a dominant position prohibited by Article 86;

Whereas, in order to carry out its duty of ensuring that the provisions of the Treaty are applied, the Commission must be empowered to address to undertakings or associations of undertakings recommendations and decisions for the purpose of bringing to an end infringements of Articles 85 and 86;

Whereas compliance with Articles 85 and 86 and the fulfilment of obligations imposed on undertakings and associations of undertakings under this Regulation must be enforceable by means of fines and periodic penalty payments;

Whereas undertakings concerned must be accorded the right to be heard by the Commission, third parties whose interests may be affected by a decision must be given the opportunity of submitting their comments beforehand, and it must be ensured that wide publicity is given to decisions taken;

Whereas all decisions taken by the Commission under this Regulation are subject to review by the Court of Justice under the conditions specified in the Treaty; whereas it is moreover desirable to confer upon the Court of Justice, pursuant to Article 172, unlimited jurisdiction in respect of decisions under which the Commission imposes fines or periodic penalty payments;

Whereas this Regulation may enter into force without prejudice to any other provisions that may hereafter be adopted pursuant to Article 87;

Has adopted this Regulation:

ARTICLE 1

Basic provision

Without prejudice to Articles 6, 7 and 23 of this Regulation, agreements, decisions and concerted practices of the kind described in Article 85(1) of the Treaty and the abuse of a dominant position in the market, within the meaning of Article 86 of the Treaty, shall be prohibited, no prior decision to that effect being required.

ARTICLE 2

Negative clearance

Upon application by the undertakings or associations of undertakings concerned, the Commission may certify that, on the basis of the facts in its possession, there are no grounds under Article 85(1) or Article 86 of the Treaty for action on its part in respect of an agreement, decision or practice.

ARTICLE 3

Termination of infringements

1. Where the Commission, upon application or upon its own initiative, finds that there is infringement of Article 85 or Article 86 of the Treaty, it may by decision require the undertakings or associations of undertakings concerned to bring such infringement to an end.

2. Those entitled to make application are:

(a) Member States;

(b) natural or legal persons who claim a legitimate interest.

3. Without prejudice to the other provisons of this Regulation, the Commission may, before taking a decision under paragraph 1, address to the undertakings or associations of undertakings concerned recommendations for termination of the infringement.

ARTICLE 4

Notification of new agreements, decisions and practices

1. Agreements, decisions and concerted practices of the kind described in Article 85(1) of the Treaty which come into existence after the entry into force of this Regulation and in respect of which the parties seek application of Article 85(3) must be notified to the Commission. Until they have been notified, no decision in application of Article 85(3) may be taken.

2. Paragraph 1 shall not apply to agreements, decisions or concerted practices where:

(1) the only parties thereto are undertakings from one Member State and the agreements, decisions or practices do not relate either to imports or to exports between Member States;

(2) not more than two undertakings are party thereto, and the agreements only:
   (a) restrict the freedom of one party to the contract in determining the prices or conditions of business upon which the goods which he has obtained from the other party to the contract may be resold, or
   (b) impose restrictions on the exercise of the rights of the assignee or user of industrial property rights – in particular patents, utility models, designs or trade marks – or of the person entitled under a contract to the assignment, or grant, of the right to use a method of manufacture or knowledge relating to the use and to the application of industrial processes;

(3) they have as their sole object:
   (a) the development or uniform application of standards or types; or
   (b) joint research and development;
   (c) specialisation in the manufacture of products, including agreements necessary for achieving this,

      — where the products which are the subject of specialisation do not, in a substantial part of the common market, represent more than 15 per cent of the volume of business done in identical products or those considered by consumers to be similar by reason of their characteristics, price and use, and
      — where the total annual turnover of the participating undertakings does not exceed 200 million units of account.

These agreements, decisions and practices may be notified to the Commission.

ARTICLE 5

Notification of existing agreements, decisions and practices

1. Agreements, decisions and concerted practices of the kind described in Article 85(1) of the Treaty which are in existence at the date of entry into force of this Regulation and in respect of which the parties seek application of Article 85(3) shall be notified to the Commission before 1 November 1962. However, notwithstanding the foregoing provisions, any agreements, decisions and concerted practices to which not more than two undertakings are party shall be notified before 1 February 1963.

2. Paragraph 1 shall not apply to agreements, decisions or concerted practices falling within Article 4(2); these may be notified to the Commission.

ARTICLE 6

Decisions pursuant to Article 85(3)

1. Whenever the Commission takes a decision pursuant to Article 85(3) of the Treaty, it shall specify therein the date from which the decision shall take effect. Such date shall not be earlier than the date of notification.

2. The second sentence of paragraph 1 shall not apply to agreements, decisions or concerted practices falling within Article 4(2) and Article 5(2), nor to those falling within Article 5(1) which have been notified within the time limit specified in Article 5(1).

ARTICLE 7

Special provisions for existing agreements, decisions and practices

1. Where agreements, decisions and concerted practices in existence at the date of entry into force of this Regulation and notified within the time limits specified in Article 5(1) do not satisfy the requirements of Article 85(3) of the Treaty and the undertakings or associations of undertakings concerned cease to give effect to them or modify them in such manner that they no longer fall within the prohibition contained in Article 85(1) or that they satisfy the requirements of Article 85(3), the prohibition contained in Article 85(1) shall apply only for a period fixed by the Commission. A decision by the

Commission pursuant to the foregoing sentence shall not apply as against undertakings and associations of undertakings which did not expressly consent to the notification.

2. Paragraph 1 shall apply to agreements, decisions and concerted practices falling within Article 4(2) which are in existence at the date of entry into force of this Regulation if they are notified before 1 January 1967.

ARTICLE 8

Duration and revocation of decisions under Article 85(3)

1 A decision in application of Article 85(3) of the Treaty shall be issued for a specified period and conditions and obligations may be attached thereto.

2. A decision may on application be renewed if the requirements of Article 85(3) of the Treaty continue to be satisfied.

3. The Commission may revoke or amend its decision or prohibit specified acts by the parties:

(a) where there has been a change in any of the facts which were basic to the making of the decision;

(b) where the parties commit a breach of any obligation attached to the decision;

(c) where the decision is based on incorrect information or was induced by deceit;

(d) where the parties abuse the exemption from the provisions of Article 85(1) of the Treaty granted to them by the decision.

In cases to which subparagraphs (b), (c) or (d) apply, the decision may be revoked with retroactive effect.

ARTICLE 9

Powers

1. Subject to review of its decision by the Court of Justice, the Commission shall have sole power to declare Article 85(1) inapplicable pursuant to Article 85(3) of the Treaty.

2. The Commission shall have power to apply Article 85(1) and Article 86 of the Treaty; this power may be exercised notwithstanding that the time limits specified in Article 5(1) and in Article 7(2) relating to notification have not expired.

3. As long as the Commission has not initiated any procedure under Articles 2, 3 or 6, the authorities of the Member States shall remain competent to apply Article 85(1) and Article 86 in accordance with Article 88 of the Treaty; they shall remain competent in this respect notwithstanding that the time limits specified in Article 5(1) and in Article 7(2) relating to notification have not expired.

ARTICLE 10

Liaison with the authorities of the Member States

1. The Commission shall forthwith transmit to the competent authorities of the Member States a copy of the application and notifications together with copies of the most important documents lodged with the Commission for the purpose of establishing the existence of infringements of Articles 85 or 86 of the Treaty or of obtaining negative clearance or a decision in application of Article 85(3).

2. The Commission shall carry out the procedure set out in paragraph 1 in close and constant liaison with the competent authorities of the Member States; such authorities shall have the right to express their views upon that procedure.

3. An Advisory Committee on Restrictive Practices and Monopolies shall be consulted prior to the taking of any decision following upon a procedure under paragraph 1, and of any decision concerning the renewal, amendment or revocation of a decision pursuant to Article 85(3) of the Treaty.

4. The Advisory Committee shall be composed of officials competent in the matter of restrictive practices and monopolies. Each Member State shall appoint an official to represent it who, if prevented from attending, may be replaced by another official.

5. The consultation shall take place at a joint meeting convened by the Commission; such meeting shall be held not earlier than 14 days after dispatch of the notice convening it. The notice shall, in respect of each case to be examined, be accompanied by a summary of the case together with an indication of the most important documents, and a preliminary draft decision.

6. The Advisory Committee may deliver an opinion notwithstanding that some of its members or their alternates are not present. A report of the outcome of the consultative

proceedings shall be annexed to the draft decision. It shall not be made public.

ARTICLE 11

Request for information

1. In carrying out the duties assigned to it by Article 89 and by provisons adopted under Article 87 of the Treaty, the Commission may obtain all necessary information from the Governments and competent authorities of the Member States and from undertakings and associations of undertakings.

2. When sending a request for information to an undertaking or association of undertakings, the Commision shall at the same time forward a copy of the request to the competent authority of the Member State in whose territory the seat of the undertaking or association of undertakings is situated.

3. In its request the Commission shall state the legal basis and the purpose of the request and also the penalties provided for in Article 15(1)(b) for supplying incorrect information.

4. The owners of the undertakings or their representatives and, in the case of legal persons, companies or firms, or of associations having no legal personality, the persons authorised to represent them by law or by their constitution shall supply the information requested.

5. Where an undertaking or association of undertakings does not supply the information requested within the time limit fixed by the Commission, or supplies incomplete information, the Commission shall by decision require the information to be supplied. The decision shall specify what information is required, fix an appropriate time limit within which it is to be supplied and indicate the penalties provided for in Article 15(1)(b) and Article 16(1)(c) and the right to have the decision reviewed by the Court of Justice.

6. The Commission shall at the same time forward a copy of its decision to the competent authority of the Member State in whose territory the seat of the undertaking or association of undertakings is situated.

ARTICLE 12

Inquiry into sectors of the economy

1. If in any sector of the economy the trend of trade between Member States, price movements, inflexibility of prices or other circumstances suggest that in the economic sector concerned competition is being restricted or distorted within the common market, the Commission may decide to conduct a general inquiry into that economic sector and in the course thereof may request undertakings in the sector concerned to supply the information necessary for giving effect to the principles formulated in Articles 85 and 86 of the Treaty and for carrying out the duties entrusted to the Commission.

2. The Commission may in particular request every undertaking or association of undertakings in the economic sector concerned to communicate to it all agreements, decisions and concerted practices which are exempt from notification by virtue of Article 4(2) and Article 5(2).

3. When making inquiries pursuant to paragraph 2, the Commission shall also request undertakings or groups of undertakings whose size suggests that they occupy a dominant position within the common market or a substantial part thereof to supply to the Commission such particulars of the structure of the undertakings and of their behaviour as are requisite to an appraisal of their position in the light of Article 86 of the Treaty.

4. Article 10(3) to (6) and Articles 11, 13 and 14 shall apply correspondingly.

ARTICLE 13

Investigations by the authorities of the Member States

1. At the request of the Commission, the competent authorities of the Member States shall undertake the investigations which the Commission considers to be necessary under Article 14(1), or which it has ordered by decision pursuant to Article 14(3). The officials of the competent authorities of the Member States responsible for conducting these investigations shall exercise their powers upon production of an authorisation in writing issued by the competent authority of the Member State in whose territory the investigation is to be

made. Such authorisation shall specify the subject matter and purpose of the investigation.

2. If so requested by the Commission or by the competent authority of the Member State in whose territory the investigation is to be made, the officials of the Commission may assist the officials of such authorities in carrying out their duties.

ARTICLE 14

Investigating powers of the Commission

1. In carrying out the duties assigned to it by Article 89 and by provisions adopted under Article 87 of the Treaty, the Commission may undertake all necessary investigations into undertakings and associations of undertakings. To this end the officials authorised by the Commission are empowered:

(a) to examine the books and other business records;
(b) to take copies of or extracts from the books and business records;
(c) to ask for oral explanations on the spot;
(d) to enter any premises, land and means of transport of undertakings.

2. The officials of the Commission authorised for the purpose of these investigations shall exercise their powers upon production of an authorisation in writing specifying the subject matter and purpose of the investigation and the penalties provided for in Article 15(1)(c) in cases where production of the required books or other business records is incomplete. In good time before the investigation, the Commission shall inform the competent authority of the Member State in whose territory the same is to be made of the investigation and of the identify of the authorised officials.

3. Undertakings and associations of undertakings shall submit to investigations by decision of the Commission. The decision shall specify the subject matter and purpose of the investigation, appoint the date on which it is to begin and indicate the penalties provided for in Article 15(1)(c) and Article 16(1)(d) and the right to have the decision reviewed by the Court of Justice.

4. The Commission shall take decisions referred to in

paragraph 3 after consultation with the competent authority of the Member State in whose territory the investigation is to be made.

5. Officials of the competent authority of the Member State in whose territory the investigation is to be made may, at the request of such authority or of the Commission, assist the officials of the Commission in carrying out their duties.

6. Where an undertaking opposes an investigation ordered pursuant to this Article, the Member State concerned shall afford the necessary asistance to the officials authorised by the Commission to enable them to make their investigation. Member States shall, after consultation with the Commission, take the necessary measures to this end before 1 October 1962.

ARTICLE 15

Fines

1. The Commission may by decision impose on undertakings or associations of undertakings fines of from 100 to 5000 units of account where, intentionally or negligently:

(a) they supply incorrect or misleading information in an application pursuant to Article 2 or in a notification pursuant to Articles 4 or 5; or

(b) they supply incorrect information in response to a request made pursuant to Article 11(3) or (5) or to Article 12, or do not supply information within the time limit fixed by a decision taken under Article 11(5); or

(c) they produce the required books or other business records in incomplete form during investigations under Articles 13 or 14, or refuse to submit to an investigation ordered by decision issued in implementation of Article 14(3).

2. The Commission may by decision impose on undertakings or associations of undertakings fines from 1000 to 1 000 000 units of account, or a sum in excess thereof but not exceeding 10 per cent of the turnover in the preceding business year of each of the undertakings participating in the infringement where, either intentionally or negligently:

(a) they infringe Article 85(1) or Article 86 of the Treaty; or

(b) they commit a breach of any obligation imposed pursuant to Article 8(1).

In fixing the amount of the fine, regard shall be had both to the gravity and to the duration of the infringement.

3. Article 10(3) to (6) shall apply.

4. Decisions taken pursuant to paragraphs 1 and 2 shall not be of a criminal law nature.

5. The fines provided for in paragraph 2(a) shall not be imposed in respect of acts taking place:

(a) after notification to the Commission and before its decision in application of Article 85(3) of the Treaty, provided they fall within the limits of the activity described in the notification;

(b) before notification and in the course of agreements, decisions or concerted practices in existence at the date of entry into force of this Regulation, provided that notification was effected within the time limits specified in Article 5(1) and Article 7(2).

6. Paragraph 5 shall not have effect where the Commission has informed the undertakings concerned that after preliminary examination it is of opinion that Article 85(1) of the Treaty applies and that application of Article 85(3) is not justified.

ARTICLE 16

Periodic penalty payments

1. The Commission may by decision impose on undertakings or associations of undertakings periodic penalty payments of from 50 to 1000 units of account per day, calculated from the date appointed by the decision, in order to compel them:

(a) to put an end to an infringement of Articles 85 to 86 of the Treaty, in accordance with a decision taken pursuant to Article 3 of this Regulation,

(b) to refrain from any act prohibited under Article 8(3);

(c) to supply complete and correct information which it has requested by decision taken pursuant to Article 11(5);

(d) to submit to an investigation which it has ordered by decision taken pursuant to Article 14(3).

2. Where the undertakings or associations of undertakings have satisfied the obligation which it was the purpose of the periodic penalty payment to enforce, the Commission may fix the total amount of the periodic penalty payment at a lower figure than that which would arise under the original decision.

3. Article 10(3) to (6) shall apply.

ARTICLE 17

Review by the Court of Justice

The Court of Justice shall have unlimited jurisdiction within the meaning of Article 172 of the Treaty to review decisions whereby the Commission has fixed a fine or periodic penalty payment; it may cancel, reduce or increase the fine or periodic penalty payment imposed.

ARTICLE 18

Unit of account

For the purposes of applying Articles 15 to 17 the unit of account shall be that adopted in drawing up the budget of the Community in accordance with Articles 207 and 209 of the Treaty.

ARTICLE 19

Hearing of the parties and of third persons

1. Before taking decisions as provided for in Articles 2, 3, 6, 7, 8, 15 and 16, the Commission shall give the undertakings or associations of undertakings concerned the opportunity of being heard on matters to which the Commission has taken objection.

2. If the Commission or the competent authorities of the Member States consider it necessary, they may also hear other natural or legal persons. Applications to be heard on the part of such persons shall, where they show a sufficient interest, be granted.

3. Where the Commission intends to give negative clearance pursuant to Article 2 or take a decision in application of Article 85(3) of the Treaty, it shall publish a summary of the relevant application or notification and invite all interested third parties to submit their observations within a time limit

which it shall fix being not less than one month. Publication shall have regard to the legitimate interest of undertakings in the protection of their business secrets.

ARTICLE 20

Professional secrecy

1. Information acquired as a result of the application of Articles 11, 12, 13 and 14 shall be used only for the purpose of the relevant request or investigation.

2. Without prejudice to the provisions of Articles 19 and 21, the Commission and the competent authorities of the Member States, their officials and other servants shall not disclose information acquired by them as a result of the application of this Regulation and of the kind covered by the obligation of professional secrecy.

3. The provisons of paragraphs 1 and 2 shall not prevent publication of general information or surveys which do not contain information relating to particular undertakings or associations of undertakings.

ARTICLE 21

Publication of decisions

1. The Commission shall publish the decisions which it takes pursuant to Articles 2, 3, 6, 7 and 8.

2. The publication shall state the names of the parties and the main content of the decision; it shall have regard to the legitimate interest of undertakings in the protection of their business secrets.

ARTICLE 22

Special provisons

1. The Commission shall submit to the Council proposals for making certain categories of agreement, decision and concerted practice falling within Article 4(2) or Article 5(2) compulsorily notifiable under Article 4 or 5.

2. Within one year from the date of entry into force of this Regulation, the Council shall examine, on a proposal from the Commission, what special provisions might be made for exempting from the provisions of this Regulation agreements,

decisions and concerted practices falling within Article 4(2) or Article 5(2).

ARTICLE 23

Transitional provisions applicable to decisions of authorities of the Member States

1. Agreements, decisions and concerted practices of the kind described in Article 85(1) of the Treaty to which, before the entry into force of this Regulation, the competent authority of a Member State has declared Article 85(1) to be inapplicable pursuant to Article 85(3) shall not be subject to compulsory notification under Article 5. The decision of the competent authority of the Member State shall be deemed to be a decision within the meaning of Article 6; it shall cease to be valid upon expiration of the period fixed by such authority but in any event not more than three years after the entry into force of this Regulation. Article 8(3) shall apply.

2. Applications for renewal of decisions of the kind described in paragraph 1 shall be decided upon by the Commission in accordance with Article 8(2).

ARTICLE 24

Implementing provisions

The Commission shall have power to adopt implementing provisions concerning the form, content and other details of applications pursuant to Articles 2 and 3 and of notifications pursuant to Articles 4 and 5, and concerning hearings pursuant to Article 19(1) and (2).

ARTICLE 25

1. As regards agreements, decisions and concerted practices to which Article 85 of the Treaty applies by virtue of accession, the date of accession shall be substituted for the date of entry into force of this Regulation in every place where reference is made in this Regulation to this latter date.

2. Agreements, decisions and concerted practices existing at the date of accession to which Article 85 of the Treaty applies by virtue of accession shall be notified pursuant to Article 5(1)

or Article 7(1) and (2) within six months from the date of accession.

3. Fines under Article 15(2)(a) shall not be imposed in respect of any act prior to notification of the agreements, decisions and practices to which paragraph 2 applies and which have been notified within the period therein specified.

4. New Member States shall take measures referred to in Article 14(6) within six months from the date of accession after consulting the Commission.

[5. The provisions of paragraphs 1 to 4 above shall apply in the same way in the case of the accession of the Hellenic Republic, the Kingdom of Spain and the Portuguese Republic.]

This regulation shall be binding in its entirety and directly applicable in all Member States.

Done at Brussels, 6 February 1962.

Amendments

Article 25 was added by the Act of 1972 concerning the conditions of Accession and the Adjustments to the Treaty, Annex I.

Para. 5 was added by the 1979 Act of the Hellenic Republic, Annex I(V)(1) and subsequently replaced by the 1985 Act of Accession of the Kingdom of Spain and the Portuguese Republic, Annex I(IV)(5).

APPENDIX IV

EEC Treaty: Competition

ARTICLE 92

1. Save as otherwise provided in this Treaty, any aid granted by a Member State or through State resources in any form whatsoever which distorts or threatens to distort competition by favouring certain undertakings or the production of certain goods shall, in so far as it affects trade between Member States, be incompatible with the common market.

2. The following shall be compatible with the common market:

(a) aid having a social character, granted to individual consumers, provided that such aid is granted without discrimination related to the origin of the products concerned;

(b) aid to make good the damage caused by natural disasters or other exceptional occurrences;

(c) aid granted to the economy of certain areas of the Federal Republic of Germany affected by the division of Germany, in so far as such aid is required in order to compensate for the economic disadvantages caused by that division.

3. The following may be considered to be compatible with the common market:

(a) aid to promote the economic development of areas where the standard of living is abnormally low or where there is serious underemployment;

(b) aid to promote the execution of an important project of common European interest or to remedy a serious disturbance in the economy of a Member State;

(c) aid to facilitate the development of certain economic activities or of certain economic areas, where such aid does not adversely affect trading conditions to an extent contrary to the common interest. However, the aids granted to shipbuilding as of 1 January 1957 shall, in so far as they serve only to compensate for the absence of customs protection, be progressively reduced under the same conditions as apply to the elimination of customs duties, subject to the provisions of this Treaty concerning common commercial policy towards third countries;

(d) such other categories of aid as may be specified by decision of the Council acting by a qualified majority on a proposal from the Commission.

ARTICLE 93

1. The Commission shall, in co-operation with Member States, keep under constant review all systems of aid existing in those States. It shall propose to the latter any appropriate measures required by the progressive development or by the functioning of the common market.

2. If, after giving notice to the parties concerned to submit their comments, the Commission finds that aid granted by a State or through State resources is not compatible with the common market having regard to Article 92, or that such aid is being misused, it shall decide that the State concerned shall abolish or alter such aid within a period of time to be determined by the Commission.

If the State concerned does not comply with this decision within the prescribed time, the Commision or any other interested State may, in derogation from the provisions of Articles 169 and 170, refer the matter to the Court of Justice direct.

On application by a Member State, the Council may, acting unanimously, decide that aid which that State is granting or intends to grant shall be considered to be compatible with the common market, in derogation from the provisions of Article 92 or from the regulations provided for in Article 94, if such a decision is justified by exceptional circumstances. If, as regards the aid in question, the Commission has already initiated the procedure provided for in the first subparagraph of this paragraph, the fact that the State concerned has made its application to the Council shall have the effect of suspending that procedure until the Council has made its attitude known.

If, however, the Council has not made its attitude known within three months of the said application being made, the Commission shall give its decision on the case.

3. The Commission shall be informed, in sufficient time to enable it to submit its comments, of any plans to grant or alter aid. If it considers that any such plan is not compatible with

the common market having regard to Article 92, it shall without delay initiate the procedure provided for in paragraph 2. The Member State concerned shall not put its proposed measures into effect until this procedure has resulted in a final decision.

ARTICLE 94

The Council may, acting by a qualified majority on a proposal from the Commission, make any appropriate regulations for the application of Articles 92 and 93 and may in particular determine the conditions in which Article 93(3) shall apply and the categories of aid exempted from this procedure.

APPENDIX V

Notice of 3 September 1986 on Agreements of Minor Importance

The Commission considers it important to facilitate cooperation between undertakings where such cooperation is economically desirable without presenting difficulties from the point of view of competition policy, which is particularly true of cooperation between small and medium-sized undertakings. To this end it published the 'Notice concerning agreements, decisions and concerted practices in the field of cooperation between undertakings' listing a number of agreements that by their nature cannot be regarded as restraints of competition. Furthermore, in the Notice concerning its assessment of certain subcontracting agreements the Commission considered that this type of contract which offers opportunities for development, in particular, to small and medium-sized undertakings is not in itself caught by the prohibition in Article 85(1). By issuing the present Notice, the Commission is taking a further step towards defining the field of application of Article 85(1), in order to facilitate cooperation between small and medium-sized undertakings. In the Commission's opinion, agreements whose effects on trade between Member States or on competition are negligible do not fall under the ban on restrictive agreements contained in Article 85(1). Only those agreements are prohibited which have an appreciable impact on market conditions, in that they appreciably alter the market position, in other words the sales or supply possibilities, of third undertakings and of users. In the present Notice the Commission, by setting quantitative criteria and by explaining their application, has given a sufficiently concrete meaning to the concept 'appreciable' for undertakings to be able to judge for themselves whether the agreements they have concluded with other undertakings, being of minor importance, do not fall under Article 85(1). The quantitative definition of 'appreciable' given by the Commission is, however, no absolute yardstick; in fact, in individual cases even agreements between undertakings which exceed these limits may still have only a negligible effect on trade between Member States or on competition, and are therefore not caught by Article 85(1). As a result of this Notice, there should no longer be any point in undertakings obtaining negative clearance, as defined by

Article 2 of Council Regulation No. 17, for the agreements covered, nor should it be necessary to have the legal position established through Commission decisions in individual cases; notification with this end in view will no longer be necessary for such agreements. However, it is doubtful whether in an individual case an agreement appreciably affects trade between Member States or competition, the undertakings are free to apply for negative clearance or to notify the agreement. In cases covered by the present Notice the Commission, as a general rule, will not open proceedings under Regulation No. 17, either upon application or upon its own initiative. Where, due to exceptional circumstances, an agreement which is covered by the present Notice nevertheless falls under Article 85(1), the Commission will not impose fines. Where undertakings have failed to notify an agreement falling under Article 85(1) because they wrongly assumed, owing to a mistake in calculating their market share or aggregate turnover, that the agreement was covered by the present Notice, the Commission will not consider imposing fines unless the mistake was due to negligence. This Notice is without prejudice to the competence of national courts to apply Article 85(1) on the basis of their own jurisdiction, although it constitutes a factor which such courts may take into account when deciding a pending case. It is also without prejudice to any interpretation which may be given by the Court of Justice of the European Communities. The Commission holds the view that agreements between undertakings engaged in the production or distribution of goods or in the provision of services generally do not fall under the prohibition of Articles 81(1) if:

— the goods or services which are the subject of the agreement (hereinafter referred to as 'the contract products') together with the participation undertakings' other goods or services which are considered by users to be equivalent in view of their characteristics, price and intended use, do not represent more than 5 per cent of the total market for such goods or services (hereinafter referred to as 'products') in the area of the common market affected by the agreement and

— the aggregate annual turnover of the participating undertakings does not exceed 200 million ECU.

The Commission also holds the view that the said agreements do not fall under the prohibition of Article 85(1) if the above mentioned market share or turnover is exceeded by not more than one tenth during two successive financial years.

For the purposes of this Notice, participating undertakings are:

(a) undertakings party to the agreement;

(b) undertakings in which a party to the agreement, directly or indirectly,

— owns more than half the capital or business assets or
— has the power to exercise more than half the voting rights, or
— has the power to appoint more than half the members of the supervisory board, board of management or bodies legally representing the undertakings, or
— has the right to manage the affairs;

(c) undertakings which directly or indirectly have in or over a party to the agreement the rights or powers listed in (b);

(d) undertakings in or over which an undertaking referred to in (c) directly or indirectly has the rights or powers listed in (b).

Undertakings in which several undertakings as referred to in (a) to (d) jointly have, directly or indirectly, the rights or powers set out in (b) shall also be considered to be participating undertakings.

In order to calculate the market share, it is necessary to determine the relevant market. This implies the definition of the relevant product market and the relevant geographical market. The relevant product market includes besides the contract products any other products which are identical or equivalent to them. This rule applies to the products of the participating undertakings as well as to the market for such products. The products in question must be interchangeable. Whether or not this is the case must be judged from the vantage point of the user, normally taking the characteristics, price and intended use of the goods together. In certain cases, however, products can form a separate market on the basis of their characteristics, their price or their intended use alone. This is true especially where consumer preferences have developed.

Where the contract products are components which are incorporated into another product by the participating undertakings, reference should be made to the market for the latter product, provided that the components represent a significant part of it. Where the contract products are components which are sold to third undertakings, reference should be made to the market for the components. In cases where both conditions apply, both markets should be considered separately.

The relevant geographical market is the area within the Community in which the agreement produces its effects. This area will be the whole common market where the contract products are regularly bought and sold in all Member States. Where the contract products cannot be bought and sold in a part of the common market, or are bought and sold only in limited quantities or at irregular intervals in such a part, that part should be disregarded.

The relevant geographical market will be narrower than the whole common market in particular where:

— the nature and characteristics of the contract product, e.g. high transport costs in relation to the value of the product, restrict its mobility; or
— movement of the contract product within the common market is hindered by barriers to entry to national markets resulting from State intervention, such as quantitative restrictions, severe taxation differentials and non-tariff barriers, e.g. type approvals or safety standard certifications. In such cases the national territory may have to be considered as the relevant geographical market. However, this will only be justified if the existing barriers to entry cannot be overcome by reasonable effort and at an acceptable cost.

Aggregate turnover includes the turnover in all goods and services, excluding tax, achieved during the last financial year by the participating undertaking. In cases where an undertaking has concluded similar agreements with various other undertakings in the relevant market, the turnover of all participating undertakings should be taken together. The aggregate turnover shall not include dealings between participating undertakings. The present Notice shall not apply where in a relevant market competition is restricted by the cumulative effects of parallel networks of similar agreements established by several manufacturers or dealers.

The present Notice is likewise applicable to decisions by associations of undertakings and to concerted practices.

APPENDIX VI

Regulation 27 (Notification)

ARTICLE 5

Transitional provisions

1. Applications and notifications submitted prior to the date of entry into force of this regulation otherwise than on the prescribed forms shall be deemed to comply with Article 4 of this regulation.

2. The Commission may require a duly completed form to be submitted to it within such time as it shall appoint. In that event, applications and notifications shall be treated as properly made only if the forms are submitted within the prescribed period and in accordance with the provisions of this regulation.

ARTICLE 6

This regulation shall enter into force on the day following its publication in the *Official Journal of the European Communities*.

This regulation shall be binding in its entirety and directly applicable in all Member States.

Done at Brussels, 3 May 1962.

FORM A/B (see pp 154–5)

Note: This form must be accompanied by an Annex containing the information specified in the attached Complementary Note.

The form and Annex must be supplied in 13 copies (one for the Commission and one for each Member State). Supply three copies of any relevant agreement and one copy of other supporting documents.

Please do not forget to complete the Acknowledgement of Receipt annexed.

If space is insufficient, please use extra pages, specifying to which item on the form they relate.

TO THE COMMISSION OF THE EUROPEAN COMMUNITIES

Directorate-General for Competition,
Rue de la Loi, 200,
B-1049 Brussels.

A. Application for negative clearance pursuant to Article 2 of Council Regulation No. 17 of 6 February 1962 relating to implementation of Article 85(1) or of Article 86 of the Treaty establishing the European Economic Community.

B. Notification of an agreement, decision or concerted practice under Article 4 (or 5) of Council Regulation No. 17 of 6 February 1962 with a view to obtaining exemption under Article 85(3) of the Treaty establishing the European Economic Community, including notifications claiming benefit of an opposition procedure.

IDENTITY OF THE PARTIES

1. Identity of applicant/notifier
Full name and address, telephone, telex and facsimile numbers, and brief description of the undertaking(s) or association(s) of undertakings submitting the application or notification.

For partnerships, sole traders or any other incorporated body trading under a business name, give, also, the name, forename(s) and address of the proprietor(s) or partner(s).

Where an application or notification is submitted on behalf of some other person (or is submitted by more than one person) the name, address and position of the representative (or joint representative) must be given, together with proof of his authority to act. Where an application or notification is submited by or on behalf of more than one persn they should appoint a joint representative (Article 1(2) and (3) of Commission Regulation No. 27).

2. Identity of any other parties
Full name and address and brief description of any other parties to the agreement, decision or concerted practice (hereinafter referred to as 'the arrangements').

State what steps have been taken to inform these other parties of this application or notification.

(This information is not necessary in respect of standard contracts which an undertaking submitting the application or notification has concluded or intends to conclude with a number of parties (e.g. a contract appointing dealers).)

Purpose of this application/ notification
(see Complementary Note)

(Please answer yes or no to the questions)

Are you asking for negative clearance alone? (See Complementary Note – Section IV, end of first paragraph – for the consequence of such a request.)

Are you applying for negative clearance, and also notifying the arrangements to obtain an exemption in case the Commission does not grant negative clearance?

Are you only notifying the arrangements in order to obtain an exemption?

Do you claim that this application may benefit from an opposition procedure?
(See Complementary Note – Sections III, IV, VI and VII and Annex 2). If you answer 'yes', please specify the Regulation and Article number on which you are relying.

Would you be satisfied with a comfort letter? (See the end of Section VII of the Complementary Note).

The undersigned declare that the information given above and in the ... pages annexed hereto is correct to the best of their knowledge and belief, that all estimates are identified as such and are their best estimates of the underlying facts and that all the opinions expressed are sincere.

They are aware of the provisions of Article 15(1)(a) of Regulation No. 17 (see attached Complementary Note).

Place and date: ......

Signatures: ....
....
....

COMMISSION OF THE EUROPEAN COMMUNITIES

Brussels ....

Directorate-General for Competition

To

Regulation 27 (FORM A/B)

ACKNOWLEDGEMENT OF RECEIPT

(This form will be returned to the address inserted above if the top half is completed in a single copy by the person lodging it)

Your application for negative clearance dated: . . . .

Your notification dated: . . . .

concerning: . . . .

Your reference: . . . .

Parties:

1. . . . .

2. . . . . and others
(There is no need to name the other undertakings party to the arrangement)

(To be completed by the Commission.)

was received on: . . . .

and registered under No. IV/: . . . .

Please quote the above number in all correspondence

COMPLEMENTARY NOTE

CONTENTS

Index